CONCEPTUAL FRAMEWORKS IN GEOGRAPHY:
CASE STUDY SUPPLEMENTS

CASE STUDIES OF THE THIRD WORLD

PS

Contents

1 **Introduction**   1
M Barke

2 **Forest Resources in Central Africa**   6
R W Critchley and T D Douglas

3 **Water Resources and River Basin Management:
The case of the Nile**   11
J R Bevan

4 **Soil Erosion in the Himalayas with Special Reference to Nepal**   16
S J Kirkby and A Mellor

5 **Commercial Agriculture in the Third World: Problems and Prospects
for Agriculture-dependent Countries**   20
F Peck

6 **Thailand and Burma (Myanma): Contrasts in Economic Development**   25
M Sill

7 **The Growth of Manufacturing in the 'Newly Industrializing' Countries
of the Third World: Television manufacture in South East Asia**   29
C S Morphet

8 **Urbanization Trends in Africa**   33
J C Sowden

9 **Inside a Third World City: Merida, Mexico**   37
M Barke

10 **Nepal: Demographic Trends and Patterns**   42
M Sill

11 **Migration in Tanzania: Testing some Basic Models**   46
M Barke and J C Sowden

12 **Tourism and the Third World**   51
L A France and J Towner

Source Material   55

Acknowledgements

The authors and publishers wish to thank all those who gave their permission to reproduce copyright material in this book. Information regarding sources is given in the captions.

Contributors

The general editor and the contributors to this book are all lecturers at Newcastle upon Tyne Polytechnic.

Where possible, the authors have attempted to use the most recent statistics. However, it should be noted that the latest data used in the 1990 World Development Report are for the year 1988 and, for some countries, earlier years. The authors would also emphasise that 'official' statistics for many LDCs should be treated as estimates rather than as precisely accurate figures.

Oliver & Boyd
Longman House
Burnt Mill
Harlow, Essex
CM20 2JE, England
and Associated Companies throughout the world
An imprint of Longman Group UK Ltd

ISBN 0 05 004479 6
First published 1991
Second impression 1992
Third impression 1993

1 Introduction

M Barke

The Third World: problems of definition

The original definition of the term 'Third World' was mainly political, referring to the group of newly independent countries which were politically aligned neither to the 'capitalist' (First World) groupings of countries nor to the socialist (Second World) grouping in the USSR and Eastern Europe. Most of the Third World therefore consisted of former colonial territories which, after the Second World War, were gaining independence and beginning to emerge as separate nations. However, the issue of political alignment has become more confused over the years for it is difficult to describe countries such as Cuba (linked to the USSR) on the one hand and Turkey (a member of NATO) on the other as non-aligned, yet both countries belong to the Third World.

There is little doubt that the increasingly popular use of the term 'Third World' has been in the economic context, the widely held view being that Third World countries are poor. Although this is largely the case, to define the Third World in terms of economic criteria alone is inadequate partly because of the diversity of economic structures and partly because it is a *range* of conditions which most adequately describe the Third World in the latter part of the twentieth century.

It is doubtful if any one country meets all of the criteria used to define the Third World. Thus, a country such as Thailand was never colonized in a formal sense (Chapter 6). Countries such as Singapore and Kuwait are not poor countries and are in fact classified as high-income economies by the World Bank but, on the grounds of their political structure, their colonial history and the existence of significant internal inequality, they still share some of the attributes of the Third World. Similarly, South Korea and Taiwan are significant industrial countries (Chapter 7), with over 30% of GDP derived from manufacturing industry (more than any other country except West Germany), but which still lag behind the more developed countries, for example, in aspects of health care provision and, in the case of the former, high levels of international debt.

The definition of the Third World adopted in this book recognizes that such a grouping of countries represents a continuum and that any attempt to draw the line of inclusion and exclusion is rather arbitrary. As our purpose is to examine and understand processes of change within the Third World, the definition used is intended to serve this purpose and therefore possesses a strong historical perspective. We therefore regard the Third World as consisting of those countries which, during the key period of global economic expansion in the nineteenth century and first half of the twentieth century, did not become industrialized. This was the period in which a truly global economy developed and during which a large number of territories were relegated to a peripheral, dependent or subordinate position in that global economy. In many cases this position was expressed in terms of a colonial relationship.

It is clear that any attempt to formulate a precise definition of the Third World is fraught with difficulty, largely because of the sheer diversity that exists within that large grouping of countries. We shall now examine this diversity in relation to dominant and emerging issues within the Third World.

Continuing and emergent issues in Third World development

(a) Poverty and debt

One of the major unifying features of the Third World is its poverty. This can be measured in a variety of ways but the most commonly used indicator is per capita GNP. In 1988 the 'poorest' country in the world was Mozambique with a per capita GNP of $100 US. The 'richest' country in the world was Switzerland with a corresponding figure of $27 500 US, 275 times as much. Figure 1.1 shows the distribution of poverty within the world as measured by this indicator. It is clear that extreme poverty characterizes much of Africa. Of the 42 countries classified as 'low-income economies' by the World Bank (less than $500 US per capita GNP), 27 are in Africa, 14 in Asia and only one (Haiti) in South and Central America. Of the 34 'lower middle-income economies ($500–2000 US per capita GNP), 14 are in South and Central America and ten in each of Africa and Asia. Of the 13 'upper middle income economies' (over $2000 US per capital GNP) six are in South and Central America, four in Asia and only three (Gabon, Libya and Algeria – all oil producers) in Africa. In contrast, however, most of the developed 'north' possesses per capita GNP figures in excess of $10 000 US (Figure 1.1).

In the early 1980s the world economy experienced a recession, followed by recovery, especially in the industrial countries. The extent to which this recovery permeated through to Third World countries varied enormously. In much of Asia, economic growth in the 1980s has been faster than in earlier periods (Chapters 6 and 7), but in Africa and South and Central America, economic decline has taken place with *real* per capita GNP (i.e. taking account of inflation) less than it was in the 1970s. An emerging issue in the 1980s which reflected such trends was the high level of debt owed by many countries in the Third World. Much of the publicity concerning debt has concentrated upon middle-income Third World countries, many of them in Latin America. In 1987 Mexico had a total external debt of $107 882 US million and Brazil $123 932 million. These countries had borrowed huge amounts of money in the 1970s to supplement their own earnings from export commodities, to invest in development schemes and social welfare. These loans were to be repaid through export earnings from agriculture and minerals (Chapter 5). In the recession of the early 1980s the real price obtained for such export commodities fell and the cost of borrowing money from abroad increased dramatically. The result was a growing volume of overseas debt.

Although the largest amounts are owed by middle-income countries, Figure 1.2 attempts to present the debt problem in a different perspective. Whilst not minimizing the massive problems of large debts, ability to repay is also of importance.

Fig. 1.1 Per Capita GNP (US)$, 1987

Therefore, as well as the absolute amount of debt, the ratio of that debt to income is of great significance. Figure 1.2 shows the ratio of debt (total external debt per capita) to income (total GNP per capita) for most Third World countries in 1987. Whilst per capita GNP is a far from perfect measure of 'income' and the measure of total debt is a simple crude aggregate sum (ignoring, for example, the different conditions and repayment periods over which loans have been made), the pattern emerging in Figure 1.2 stresses the plight of many African countries. To be poor is unfortunate: to be in debt is

equally undesirable. But to be both poor and in debt is to experience a compounded set of problems.

(b) Human welfare

There are many objections to using GNP as a measure of relative levels of income and certainly of development. First, it assumes that data on population levels and market transactions are both available and accurate. This is unlikely to be equally the case for every country in the world. Secondly, it is a measure that can only really be applied satisfactorily to

Fig. 1.2 Third World Indebtedness: Ratio of Debt to Income

capitalist market economies. Subsistence economies, or those where transactions take place on some basis other than cash, are not adequately represented by such a measure. Thirdly, it is simply a crude average statistic and therefore ignores inequalities *within* countries, either between different groups or different regions (Chapters 8,10,12). Finally, it is purely an economic measure and development may be measured equally well or even better by indicators of improvement in human welfare.

Space does not permit a full consideration of the elements involved in human welfare. However, a useful, if selective, index of human welfare has been devised by M.D. Morris, called the Physical Quality of Life Index (PQLI). This index is formed from the three indicators of infant mortality levels, life expectancy and the degree of literacy. These three are combined into a single score with a value near 100 indicating a high PQLI. Figure 1.3 maps the PQLI scores across the world for the early 1980s. Tropical Africa and parts of South Asia stand out with low levels whilst conditions appear to be better in Central and South America. Comparing Figures 1.1 and 1.3 it is clear that there is a general association between high per capita GNP and high PQLI. However, Tanzania with a per capita GNP in 1988 of $160 US has a PQLI of 56.6 whilst Somalia with a GNP of $170 US has a PQLI of 32.3. Kenya with a higher per capita GNP of $370 US has a PQLI similar to that of Tanzania, scoring 52.2. Perhaps the greatest anomalies occur in the oil-producing states. Kuwait, Libya, Saudi Arabia, Oman and Gabon have per capita GNPs of $13 400, $1760, $6200, $5000 and $2970 respectively. Their PQLIs are, in the same order, 76.4, 51.8, 39.4, 30.8 and 30.0.

Although there may well be a broad relationship across the globe between high per capita GNP and the achievement of a high PQLI, the latter is not necessarily entirely dependent upon the former. Table 1.1 shows for a selection of Third World countries some of the variation which does take place

in the three indicators used to calculate the PQLI and how these sometimes do not relate to per capita GNP. Considerable improvements in human welfare are possible, even without major increases in GNP. Countries such as Jamaica, Thailand and Nicaragua show relatively high levels of welfare despite quite modest income levels. Even more remarkable, despite the present tragic internal strife, is Sri Lanka. Elsewhere, quite high income levels (by Third World standards) produce highly varied welfare results. Note the contrast between South Korea and Gabon for example and, to a slightly lesser degree, between Saudi Arabia and Oman. Perhaps the most remarkable figures of all are those attributed to China, but arguably, these have been achieved at the cost of political freedom and as a result of a high degree of centralized control.

As with income, internal inequalities may exist in human welfare within a country (Chapters 10, 11). Table 1.1 draws attention to one aspect of such inequality – the differences between men and women.

(c) Women and development
Only in the decade of the 1980s did the fundamental role of women in development begin to be officially recognized. Table 1.1 shows that widely different life chances are available to women compared with men in many Third World countries. The role of women in development has been emphasised in the 'basic needs' approach, that is an approach which, rather than stressing large-scale development projects (Chapter 3), is concerned with sustainable development and with meeting a family's basic requirements such as food, clothing and shelter. Access to essential services such as clean water, health and education therefore become of paramount importance. As it is women who, in many Third World countries, are responsible for a large part of food production, for supplying water and for providing the rudimentary and initial needs of the family in terms of health and education, the importance of women to this

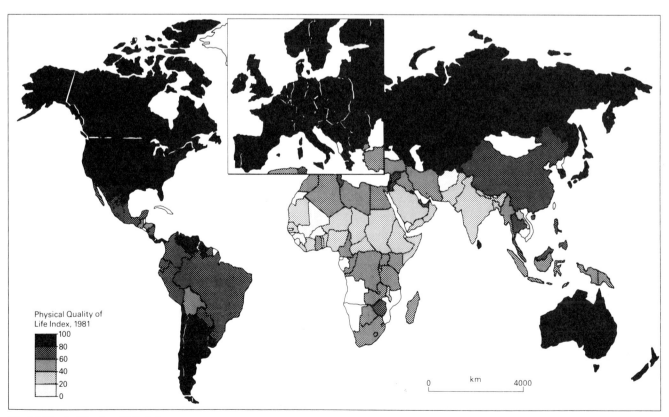

Fig. 1.3 Physical Quality of Life Index

Table 1.1 Selected countries: physical quality of life measures, 1987

Country	Per capita GNP (US) $ 1988	Life expectancy	Infant mortality (per 1000 live births)	Adult literacy Male	Adult literacy Female	Secondary education Females per 100 males
Bangladesh	170	51	118	33	22	45
Tanzania	160	53	104	93	88	66
China	330	70	31	69	55	69
Nigeria	290	51	103	42	31	33
Sri Lanka	420	71	21	91	83	106
Bolivia	570	53	108	74	65	86
Egypt	660	63	83	44	30	68
Nicaragua	830	64	60	*61	*60	168
Thailand	1000	65	30	91	88	100
Congo, People's Rep.	910	53	117	63	55	76
Jamaica	1070	73	11	+90	+93	105
Mexico	1760	69	46	90	88	88
Korea, Rep.	3600	70	24	96	88	87
Gabon	2970	53	101	62	53	81
Oman	5000	64	38	47	12	65
Saudi Arabia	6200	64	69	71	31	66
USA	19840	76	10	99	99	97

* 1984   + 1985

(Source: World Bank: *World Development Report, 1990*)

'basic needs' approach to development is obvious.

The extent to which women can play a positive and active role in producing these basic needs is itself influenced by their position in society. Figure 1.4 attempts to give a broad global summary of the position of women by summing the ranking of countries on four indicators. The ratio of females aged 0 to 4 years per 100 males in the same age group is a broad general indicator of the relative survival chances of female babies in different countries. Female life expectancy, the rate of maternal mortality and finally the ratio of females to males attending primary education complete the index.

There is a broad belt of low quality of life for women across the northern part of Africa and, extending into South Asia. India, Bangladesh and Nepal are the only countries where female life expectancy is less than that of males. No South or Central American country falls into the lowest category, indicating that the quality of life for women in such countries is rather better than in other parts of the Third World. In some of the poorest countries in the world the position of women is doubly unfortunate. They are disadvantaged because they are poor but they are further disadvantaged because they are women.

Nevertheless, female life chances are not always directly attributable to poverty. In poor countries such as Chad and Ethiopia female life expectancy is less than 50 years but in other poor countries, for example China and Sri Lanka, it exceeds 70 years. Low quality of life for women cannot be explained solely by poverty, therefore, and it is clear that in many parts of the Third World cultural factors and religious attitudes are equally important.

As development has progressed, the roles of women in a number of countries have changed. For example, in some parts of Asia and Latin America, the proportion of women engaged in manufacturing industry is high. This is especially so in small countries such as Singapore, where 56% of its manufacturing labour force is female. Many of these activities are in labour-intensive export-oriented industries such as electronics. However, in other parts of the Third World women are excluded from many economic activities. For example, in the developed West, most typists are female. In a country such as India they would be much more likely to be male. In contrast, women's share of agricultural work across the Third World is high. Highest levels are found in those societies where agriculture is subsistence based or engaged in production for local markets. Where agriculture is increasingly commercialized, the level of male participation tends to increase. Nevertheless, it is the case that the majority of the Third World's farmers are women and it is they who therefore have the closest direct contact with many aspects of the environment and its management. This leads into our fourth and final theme – the emerging environmental crisis in the Third World.

(d) Environmental issues

Although much had previously been written on environmental issues it was in the decade of the 1980s, and especially with the publication of the Bruntland Report, that the environment became a phenomenon of global concern for all. The last decade has seen a growing realization that we live in an *interdependent* world where events in one part of the planet have significant repercussions elsewhere. Three often inter-related issues are increasingly prominent – the prospect of global climatic change, land degradation (Chapters 2 and 4), and environmental disasters. These are all threats to environmental sustainability, now recognized as an essential component of sustainable development. The burden of such problems falls most heavily upon the poorest countries and upon the poor within those countries. We also have to face the unpleasant fact that, far from being 'natural' events or 'acts of God' many such environmental problems are directly attributable to human activities. Not only are we responsible for many environmental problems, but presumably, by modifying our behaviour, we should be able to moderate their severity.

In traditional societies the environment is often seen as something to be nurtured, to avoid taking risks with and which should be passed on to future generations in a state which will facilitate continuity. Under capitalist and Marxist economic development, however, the environment is often viewed as something that must be 'conquered' and used for high levels of

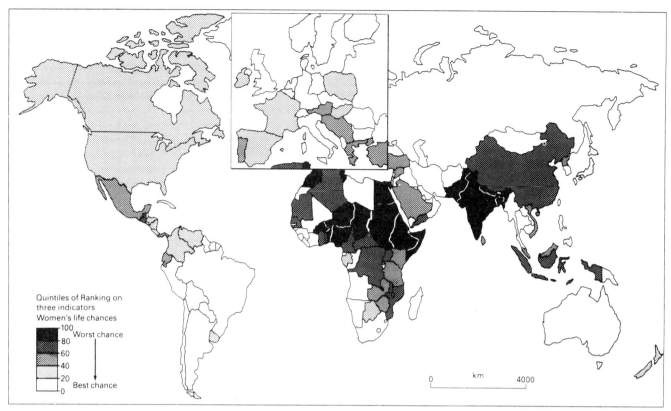

Fig. 1.4 Women's Life Chances on Four Indicators

production and for monetary gain often using expensive advanced technology. All too often, this leads to abuse. It is perhaps in regions such as the tropical rain forests where such conflicts are seen most clearly.

Consideration of environmental issues in the Third World leads one to the necessity of examining the inter-connectedness of global systems, for example, the relationship between the destruction of the great forests, the hydrological cycle, and climatic change. Figure 1.5 shows the main components of environmental degradation, the complex set of linkages that exist between these components, and the principal environmental issues in the contemporary Third World.

Given such linkages it is hardly surprising that many parts of the Third World experience frequent disasters. Tragic events such as those at the Union Carbide plant in Bhopal, India, in 1984 come readily to mind but the two most frequent disasters are famine and flood and are both related to the complex interaction between natural phenomena and mismanagement of the environment. Yet the victims of such mismanagement are rarely themselves the principal cause. In many cases, the problems of land degradation are attributed to the pressure of a rising population on a limited resource base but, in circumstances of extreme poverty, peasant farmers have to rely on their own labour and that of their family to increase output. It is scarcely surprising, therefore, that large families are associated with poverty. Another child may represent another mouth to feed but it also represents another pair of hands. But with higher population densities comes the need to utilize more land. Much of it may be marginal in terms of its productivity or ecologically marginal and lacking in resilience when vegetation is cleared. Where deforestation takes place, so too does soil erosion. Run-off increases and floods may result (Chapter 4). However, those who are forced on to such marginal areas are often forced there through poverty, political circumstances or population pressure and

have no resources other than their own labour to devote to the effective management of such environments.

In this way, the economic marginalization of the poor is linked to environmental degradation. This applies at the regional scale within countries and also on a global scale. It is one of the major underlying themes of this collection of case studies that Third World problems cannot be understood in isolation, they are not an individual and unique product of a specific country or region. Many Third World problems are a product of the inter-connected world in which we live, whether they be problems relating to poverty, welfare, gender or the environment.

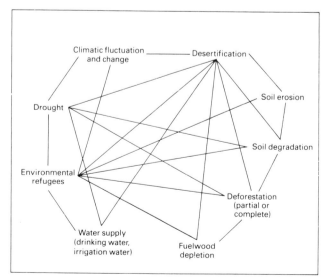

Fig. 1.5 Components and Linkages in Environmental Degradation

2 Forest Resources in Central Africa

R W Critchley and T D Douglas

Introduction

The geographical distribution of natural resources is obviously an important factor influencing any region's potential for development. Perhaps the most fundamental resource of all is land and its productive potential. A second resource which has grown to a huge level of importance in the last two centuries is energy. In many Third World countries demographic pressure has, in turn, increased the pressure on land for cultivation purposes and additional energy. In many parts of Africa and Asia firewood and other traditional fuels account for up to 90% of energy consumption. It is clear that, with very rapid rates of population increase, wood may be cut for all sorts of uses faster than it can be grown. Where this happens the resource is said to be 'non-sustainable'. Table 2.1 shows the position in Africa, and whilst the situation is most severe in arid and semi-arid areas, where vegetation growth can be slow, many regions with considerable resources of tropical forests are also showing deficits or potential deficits. If the rates of fuelwood consumption of the early 1980s continue, the fuelwood deficit will double by the year 2000.

This chapter will examine the situation, not in the most frequently cited arid and semi-arid regions of Africa, but in a region where the current state of affairs appears to be less critical but where, if current trends continue, forest resources may be depleted to a dangerous extent. We are concerned here with the increasing demands being placed on the moist tropical forest areas of central Africa. The spectacular deforestation of similar areas in South America has received much attention in the last few years. Less spectacular but equally worrying trends are under way in central Africa. As we shall see later in this chapter, deforestation owes its origins to a variety of causes and is not solely a product of increasing demands for fuelwood for cooking, heating, lighting and manufacturing processes.

Tropical moist forests

The fullest expression of vegetation growth occurs when temperature and humidity conditions are most favourable and takes the form of closed forest (i.e. where the crowns of the trees touch) which contains a mixture of evergreen and semi-deciduous species of broad-leaved trees. The conditions necessary for development include not less than 100 mm of rainfall in any month for two out of three years, a mean annual temperature of 24 °C and freedom from frost. Such conditions occur around the equator at altitudes below 1300 metres and are found in three major regions on the globe: South America (the Amazon basin), south-east Asia (Malaysia and Indonesia) and in tropical Africa coinciding with the moist tropical climatic zone. In Africa there are three centres, the coastal Guinean Rain Forest, the Congo Rain Forest, around the Zaire river and the Malagasy Rain Forest (the eastern coastal strip of Madagascar) (Figure 2.1).

A study by FAO of 37 African countries revealed that in 1980 there were 216 million hectares of closed forests in tropical Africa of which more than 80% are in central Africa with some 50% lying in Zaire alone. If undisturbed forest is considered, then the relative values are 95% and 68% respectively.

Closed broad-leaved forests are diverse, stratified systems which have developed during the climatic changes occurring since the Quaternary Ice Ages, and it has been estimated that moist forests worldwide support 50% of all the world's plant and animal species. The upper canopy in such systems is about 30 metres high and dense enough to shade the ground so that grasses fail to grow. Where soils are drier, or at higher altitudes, the trees are somewhat shorter and the system may be described as scrub forest or thicket. In areas north and south of this zone, where a short dry season occurs, less leaching of soil nutrients takes place and the forests that develop are simpler, less diverse and can be described as moist semi-deciduous. Although a minimum annual rainfall exceeding 1350 mm and a dry season not exceeding two to three months is normally considered essential for the development of moist

Table 2.1 Fuelwood deficits in Africa

Fuelwood situation	Countries mainly affected
Acute scarcity (Available supplies of fuelwood insufficient to meet minimum requirements)	Burkino Faso, Chad, Mali, Mauritania, Niger, Sudan, Kenya, Ethiopia, Somalia, Botswana, Namibia.
Deficit (Fuelwood supplies consumed faster than they are replenished by natural regeneration and forest growth)	Cameroon (north), Congo (central), Zaire (west and south), Malawi, Madagascar, Uganda, Tanzania, Togo, The Gambia, Guinea, Benin, Senegal, Sierra Leone, Nigeria, Mozambique.
Prospective deficit (If present trends continue, fuelwood supplies will be in deficit by the year 2000)	Ghana, Ivory Coast, The Central African Republic, Angola, Zimbabwe, Guinea, Bissau.
Surplus potential for wood-based energy	Cameroon (south), Congo (west and north), Equatorial Guinea, Angola (part), Zaire (central).

(Source: WRI/IIED, 1986)

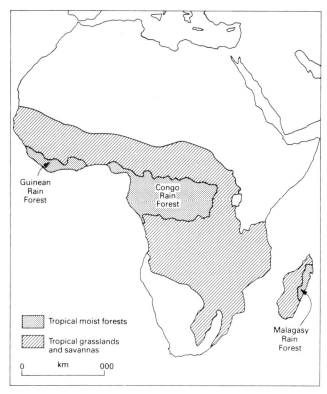

Fig. 2.1 Distribution of Tropical Moist Forest in Africa

Table 2.2 Areas of closed forest and rates of deforestation in selected tropical African countries

Country	Area of closed forest, x 10³ ha 1980	Rate of deforestation x 10³ ha per year 1980
Group 1		
Ivory Coast	4 907	290
Guinea	2 072	36
Group 2		
Cameroon	18 105	80
Congo	21 508	22
Zaire	105 975	182
Group 3		
Benin	47	1
Guinea Bissau	664	17
Group 4		
Central African Republic	3 595	5
Sierra Leone	798	6

Group 1   Large areas being lost at higher than average rate.
Group 2   Large areas being lost at lower than average rate.
Group 3   Small areas of forest intact with higher than average loss rates.
Group 4   Small areas of forest intact with lower than average loss rates.

(Source: WRI/IIED, 1986)

forest, regional differences may prevail to allow their development. For instance in Gabon the dry season may reach six months, but because of the presence of a permanent cloud cover during that season, humidity remains high.

The rate of production of new plant material (biomass) by the process of photosynthesis in all forests represents the highest of all land-based vegetation, accounting for 66% of the total fixation of carbon dioxide by solar energy. Tropical forests account for some 75% of this total; hence the environmental concern associated with deforestation. The major producers in moist forests are large trees with standing biomasses of the order of over 100 tonnes per hectare. The dominance of individual tree species is, however, low, producing a very diverse canopy and creating sub-canopy conditions in which thrive smaller trees, creepers and herbs. In the lower layers of the canopy stand numerous small seedlings and saplings awaiting a break in the canopy, caused perhaps by the death of a tree due to lightning, windfall or old age, before growing rapidly in an attempt to fill the gap. The forest consists, then, of a mosaic of mature stages, gaps created by falling trees and building phases; the traditional stratified model encountered in the literature refers largely to the mature phase of forests. Estimates of areas of moist tropical forest and rates of loss in a number of African countries are given in Table 2.2.

Causes of deforestation

Deforestation is widely held to be a problem of major environmental significance. A recent estimate of the area of deforestation in Africa was 1.3 million hectares per year. The process arises from a wide range of causes:
(a) Clearance for agriculture. Human population growth is the major trigger in the search for new land on which to produce food. In the lands at the margin of the forest, such as Rwanda and Benin, the vast majority of land is already used

for agriculture and very few forests remain. In the surviving extensive areas of virgin (primary) forest in central Africa (notably Congo and Zaire), the progress of clearance is limited by inaccessibility. Over large parts of Africa, slash-and-burn agriculture is practised. The initial burning of forest provides a nutrient-rich soil for cropping for a few years, but is followed by a rapid decline in fertility and then abandonment. Only limited regrowth of forest may take place and in many places irreparable environmental damage may result.
(b) Fuelwood. Fuelwood is the primary source of energy for many urban households and for virtually all rural households in Africa. In many areas, the removal of fuelwood from forests exceeds the rate at which the forests can regenerate. This situation is at its most acute in areas around towns and cities where an expanding circle of deforestation can be recognized, particularly along roadsides.
(c) Commercial logging. The removal of timber as a cash crop is locally important. This represents a resource which Third World countries can use to earn foreign currency. The Ivory Coast and Congo are two good African examples. Compared with the volume of forests destroyed through clearance for agriculture usage, this activity is of secondary importance.

The consequences of deforestation

The issue of tropical deforestation has received considerable media coverage during the 1980s. In arguments over what should or could be done to combat current trends, it is important to keep in sight the various consequences of deforestation.
(a) Fuelwood collection. With depleted forest reserves the search for fuelwood incurs greater time on the part of those whose job it is to collect fuel (usually women). Rarely is it feasible to substitute another fuel for wood, as electricity is not usually available in rural areas and petroleum products are too expensive. Fuelwood is effectively free in rural areas. Sometimes animal dung and crop residues are used as fuel to the detriment of soil fertility where they could be more profitably employed.
(b) Depletion of soil nutrients. Deforestation is invariably

7

accompanied by a rapid depletion of soil nutrients as they are leached out and no longer retained in the above-ground biomass.

(c) Soil erosion. As a result of forest clearance, surface run-off of rainwater is measurably greater and this can often lead to soil erosion, flooding and silting of water courses and reservoirs (Chapter 4). Local water tables are also lowered which may have major effects on crop yields. In extreme cases desertification may result as humidity and rainfall decrease.

(d) Biological diversity. Many ecologists have noted that the destruction of tropical moist forests will reduce the biological diversity of our planet by reducing its genetic base, resulting in the partial loss of a valuable resource for plant breeders and perhaps for medical researchers too.

(e) 'Greenhouse' effect. At a global level, the most alarming predictions have pointed to the role of tropical moist forests in absorbing carbon dioxide (CO_2) during photosynthesis so helping to limit its effect as a greenhouse gas. The 'greenhouse' effect is the raising of air temperatures due to the heat retaining properties of several gaseous emissions of which CO_2 represents about 50% of the total. (CFCs and nitrous oxides are other important greenhouse gases.) The threat is that the greenhouse effect will lead to global warming with unpredictable climatic effects, including the possibility of melting polar ice caps with

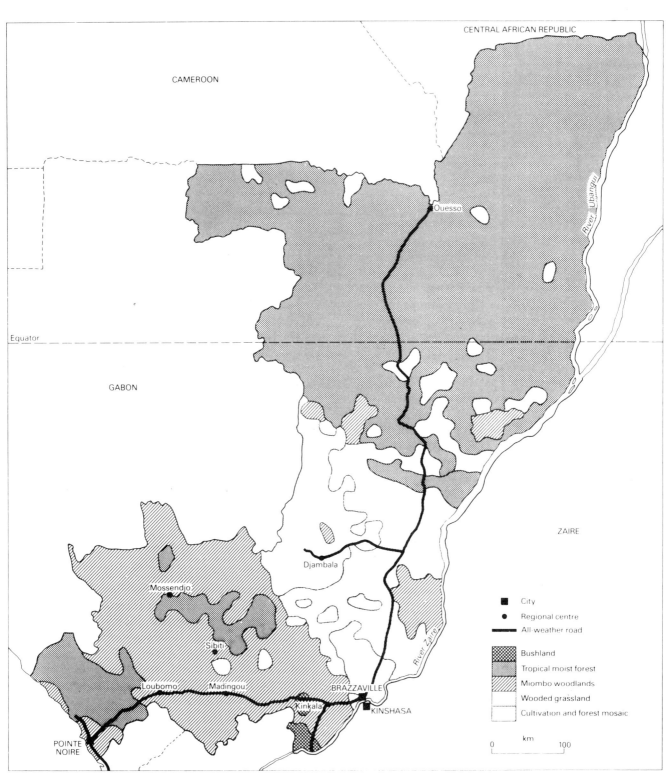

Fig. 2.2 People's Republic of Congo: Major Biomass Classes Derived from Remotely Sensed Data

the devastating consequence of worldwide sea-level rises. Scientists argue about the likely extent of this effect and its timing, but many environmentalists are alarmed at the prospect for the next century. By the absorption, retention and emission of CO_2, tropical forests play a major role in the carbon cycle. Their destruction releases previously stored carbon into the atmosphere and limits the further amount of carbon which can be stored in the biomass rather than as atmospheric CO_2.

Estimating woody biomass in The People's Republic of Congo

Woody biomass consists of trees, shrubs and bushes, including trunks, branches and twigs. It can be measured in tonnes per hectare and the yearly biomass production (mean annual increment) in tonnes per hectare per year. This annual increment represents the new growth of wood, and is relevant to ideas of sustainability and the maintenance of biomass. For instance an area in which woody biomass is being extracted at a rate greater than the annual increment will be undergoing deforestation.

Estimates of non-commercial wood such as fuelwood are notoriously difficult to obtain. Only in urban areas where most of the population does not have access to free wood supplies does fuelwood become part of the commercial scene. In rural areas it is regarded as a free good to be collected for domestic consumption or traded with nearby urban areas. Given the problems of quantifying woody biomass and the potential threats being posed by widespread deforestation, there is an urgent need for techniques which can give an assessment of woody biomass. Satellite remote sensing has recently been used to provide some of the answers to this problem. Earth resource satellites equipped with radiometers (e.g. Landsat) and meteorological satellites (e.g. NOAA, METEOSAT) collect a vast amount of information about the land surface. These instruments detect radiation in the visible and infrared wavelengths. Green vegetation has a high reflectance in the near infrared waveband and a low reflectance in the red waveband. Remote sensing experts have used these properties to give a 'vegetation index' for the land surface. This vegetation index is in effect a measure of vegetation production rate and can be interpreted to estimate the area of different vegetation types. As this can be repeated on a frequent basis (sometimes

daily), the opportunity now exists to map vegetation characteristics and changes in even the most remote regions.

The People's Republic of Congo lies astride the equator in central Africa. It contains a variety of vegetation types including a large but remote and inaccessible area of tropical moist forest. The country's population is 1.91 million (1986) growing at an annual rate of 3.8%. Most of the population is located in the south of the country in a strip between Brazzaville (595 000 inhabitants), the capital, and Pointe Noire (297 000 inhabitants), the centre of the oil industry. Timber and associated forest products were the greatest source of the country's revenue until 1972 when oil took over. Forty-five per cent of the population live in urban areas, one of the highest proportions in Africa.

Figure 2.2 shows an interpretation of the biomass classes based on remotely sensed information. The area of each of these classes is given in Table 2.3. It can be seen from the map that Brazzaville lies in an area where biomass supply is limited. Surprisingly, for a location so near the equator, there are extensive wooded grasslands (savanna) and relatively thin woodlands. Plate 2.1 illustrates the wooded grassland found 30 km north of Brazzaville and Plate 2.2 shows the mosaic of grassland and small patches of forest north of Brazzaville near the Gabon border. This pattern is the product of poor soils on plateau areas and slash-and-burn agriculture.

Given the limited forest resources identified by remote sensing for the central part of The People's Republic of Congo and the current concern (in the developed world at least) about the effects of the depletion of tropical forest, it is interesting to discuss the options of forest policy which are open to such a Third World country.

It is difficult to assess the amount and causes of deforestation in The People's Republic of Congo. Satellite remote sensing will enable monitoring to take place but little reliable information exists as to the extent of forests in the past. What does seem clear, however, is that in the vicinity of the capital, Brazzaville, there has been considerable deforestation and thinning of woodlands. Some forests close to the city have disappeared entirely. Further afield, slash-and-burn agriculture stimulated in part by the demographic trends has undoubtedly been responsible for large losses of trees. This is particularly the case in the 'cultivation and forest mosaic' class identified in Figure 2.2. As more of the existing forests are cleared for

Plate 2.1: The vegetation north of Brazzaville near the Gabon border at 2° south of the equator. The woody species are confined to the least accessible slopes and the valley bottom, whilst the extensive plateau areas are largely grassland. Regular burning and fuelwood collections are depleting these resources.

Plate 2.2: The wooded grassland found 30km north of Brazzaville. Note the relatively low density of trees in this savanna. This area is regularly burnt and cultivated for cassava and millet.

agriculture, projected fuelwood demand could exceed sustainable production of the remaining forests over an ever increasing area.

Any forestry policy should take account of all the competing demands on trees. One development which has been tried on a limited scale is peri-urban plantations. These are managed plantations of quick-growing species such as pine and eucalyptus on the fringe of cities which are harvested to supply fuelwood and timber products to the urban area. Another possibility is to establish forest reserves in areas of existing forest in which slash-and-burn agriculture is not permitted. Both of these solutions, however, do not involve the local people to any great extent. A concept termed 'social forestry' may yield better results in the long term. This aims to encourage villagers and agriculturalists to plant trees and to manage them on a local village or farm scale. This represents a very different approach from the traditional slash-and-burn, and in the absence of programmes of education and much better communications would be hard to encourage on a sufficiently large scale to have much impact.

Another approach is to tackle the problem from the point of view of fuelwood consumption. Fuelwood prices in Brazzaville are already high in comparison with many African cities (partly the result of the very high transport and distribution costs resulting from the poor road network). As these costs continue to rise and represent a higher proportion of household budgets, higher priorities may be placed on the more efficient use of fuelwoods. Studies in The People's Republic of Congo and numerous other Third World countries have demonstrated that significant savings in fuelwoods can be made (thus reducing the demand for forest products) when more fuel-efficient stoves are used. For instance, many domestic fires merely comprise an open wood fire surrounded by three stones on which a pot is balanced. The dissemination of appropriate cooking stove technology can therefore contribute to a lowering of fuelwood demand.

Conclusion

It is difficult to predict likely trends in the forest resources of The People's Republic of Congo. The great swathe of tropical forest in the north of the country is not under any immediate threat as it is too remote and contains very sparse human populations. The forests in the west of the country are more accessible and are being depleted by logging operations and as a result of expansion of fuelwood cutting. Around Brazzaville in the woodlands and grasslands and existing remnants of forests, the pattern of a declining forest resource is likely to continue in the absence of major changes in the traditional land-uses and with the continuing use of low-efficiency fires for cooking.

Table 2.3 Characteristics of biomass classes in the Congo

Biomass class	Area (x 10^5 ha)	Growing stock (tonnes/ha)	Annual increment (tonnes/ha (per year)
1. **Wooded grassland** Low biomass areas with extensive grasslands and a few scattered trees.	23.2	2.0	0.1
2. **Bushland** Areas of low growing shrubs and thickets.	6.5	28.0	0.7
3. **Miombo woodlands** Relatively thin woodlands: this is an important vegetation type in southern Africa.	71.4	40.0	0.4
4. **Cultivation & forest mosaic** Areas where forests and woodlands have been disturbed by agriculture; often secondary regrowth.	55.7	43.0	1.0
5. **Tropical moist forest** Closed forests, usually with very sparse human populations.	181.9	95.0	1.2

ASSIGNMENTS

1. (a) Using the data shown in Table 2.3, calculate the total growing stock and annual increment for the Congo for each biomass class (tonnes).
   (b) Use these figures to find the total growing stock and annual increment for the whole country.
   (c) Using the Figure 2.2, estimate the annual increment within a sector of radius 100 km centred on Brazzaville (1 km² = 100 ha).
   (d) Taking a population of 750 000 within this sector, and a typical per capita fuelwood consumption of 320 kg (0.32 tonne) per year; estimate the fuelwood demand for the sector.
   (e) Assuming that this 100 km radius sector supplies fuelwood to the Brazzaville area, compare the annual increment of biomass calculated in (c) above (the potential sustainable supply) with the estimate of consumption in (d). On this simple basis, do you think that Brazzaville is likely to have a fuelwood problem? What would be the situation if the realistic radius for fuelwood supply and collection were 50 km or even 30 km?

2. Why do you think fuelwood is such an important source of energy in Africa?

3. Assuming current rates of deforestation for the African countries in Table 2.2, calculate how long it would take to reduce the 1980 areas of closed forests by one half.

3 Water Resources and River Basin Management

J R Bevan

The case of the Nile

Introduction

The importance of water resources in the development process was highlighted by the declaration from the United Nations that the 1980s be labelled the 'International Drinking Water Supply and Sanitation Decade'. The need for this declaration was only too obvious with three out of five people in the Third World having no easy access to clean water, and four-fifths of diseases in such countries being linked to dirty water and lack of sanitation. The problem of water supply is not an absolute global one, but is most certainly one of distribution and timing. Water is often available at the wrong places at the wrong times. Within the hydrological cycle, it is the precipitation, run-off and groundwater storage elements which provide most possibilities for water management; and it is the manipulation and use of rivers which is usually most central to the successful development of water resources in a country.

Table 3.1 demonstrates the uneven availability of run-off in the major continents and if run-off is calculated as a percentage of precipitation, it becomes evident that Africa is the most disadvantaged continent. Nearly 50% of the continent's surface run-off is concentrated in the Zaire Basin alone and about 75% in the eight basins of the Zaire, Niger, Ogooue, Zambesi, Nile, Sanga, Chari Lagone and Volta (42.7% of Africa's area). Thus nearly 60% of Africa's area remains with only 25% of the surface water resources (although this excludes the natural lakes). The optimum use of these major rivers is of paramount importance, especially when rainfall throughout much of Africa is unreliable. The difficulties are compounded where major rivers cross international boundaries and the Nile is examined in this chapter as a good example of the issues faced in river management on a grand scale.

The present dilemma of providing good quality water to the population, agriculture and industries of the Third World is one which typifies the current environmental, social and economic trap in which the lesser developed countries often find themselves. The estimated cost of 'clean water for all by 1990' by the UN was between $300 billion and $600 billion, yet spending in the early 1980s was only between $6 billion

and $7 billion per year. This lack of finance, together with lack of available skilled labour, means that low-cost, self-help schemes would, perhaps, provide the most likely short-term solution. This contrasts with a number of very large reservoir schemes which have been developed in the Third World during the last thirty years.

The numerous purposes to which a large dam can be put, together with its visible presence as a symbol of modernity and apparent mastery over nature, has led to the building of a number of these large structures. Many have had unforeseen problems, such as the resettlement problems of the Kainji and Akosombo Dams, the seismic effects of the Kariba and the concern over who will purchase the vast HEP resources of the new Itaipu Dam on the Parana. However, it is the Aswan High Dam which perhaps best illustrates the successes and failures of a large-scale dam project on a major river.

The Nile

The Nile and its tributaries represent the longest river courses in the world, nearly 6700 km long, passing through nine countries and a wide range of climates (Figure 3.1). It is unique as a major river flowing south to north through these latitudes with a basin area of about 3 million km^2; and it is unique in its water resource development history, stretching back 7000 years. Despite the huge hydrological and engineering developments in all that time and especially in this century, the management of the entire basin is still fraught with difficulties. Egypt and Sudan are the main users and these two countries have developed more control structures than those further south, although it is the south which provides most of the rainfall.

Figure 3.1 shows the changing patterns of precipitation, evaporation and discharge throughout the course of the Nile, together with the main storage and control structures which have been erected. In the southern headwaters, the major lakes play an important role in the hydrology of the upper reaches and Lake Victoria, in particular, has been studied in association with climatic change and Nile discharges. The Owen Falls Dam in Uganda, constructed in 1954, has a huge long-term storage capacity, but is used primarily for Hydro Electric Power (HEP) generation. The smaller lakes and swamps around Lake Kioga lose more water by evaporation than they gain by rainfall, so that the discharge of the Bahr el Jebel (upper White Nile) in southern Sudan is little more than the flow leaving Lake Victoria. It totals about 31.4 milliards (10^9 m^3) per annum at Mongalla, with a fairly even annual regime (Figure 3.1). The main tributary entering from the west is the Bahr el Ghazal which enters the huge Sudd region, where massive evaporation losses take place from an ecologically unique area. The construction of the Jonglei canal by diverting water from the Sudd is intended to save a large proportion of

Table 3.1 Average annual water balance of the continents (volumes in 10^9 m^3)

Continent	Precipitation	Evaporation	Run-off
Africa	20 700	17 300	3 400
Asia	30 700	18 500	12 200
Australia	7 100	4 700	2 400
Europe	6 600	3 800	2 800
N America	15 600	9 700	5 900
S America	28 000	16 900	11 100
Antarctica	2 400	400	2 000
Total land areas	111 100	71 300	39 800

(Source: Saha & Barrow, 1982)

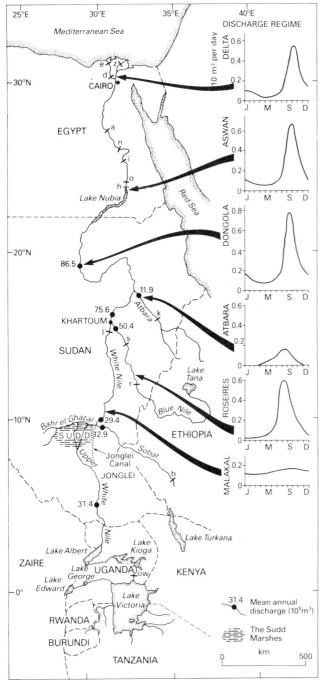

Annual average discharge or evaporation loss (10^9m^3)	PLACE	PRECIPITATION (mm)	EVAPORATION (mm)	CAPACITY (10^9m^3) STORAGE/CONTROL
	MEDITERRANEAN COAST	200	1100	
	NILE DELTA	25–200	840	DELTA (d), ZIFTA (z) & EDFINA (e) BARRAGES
67	CAIRO	25	1020	BARRAGES
	ASSIUT (a)	NA	NA	BARRAGE
	NAGA HAMMAD (n) & ISNA (i)			BARRAGES
(−17)	ASWAN	0.5	1640	OLD ASWAN (o) & HIGH ASWAN (h) (storage & energy) (5) (115)
86	(White Nile)			
	JEBEL AULIA (j)	200	2840	STORAGE DAM (3.6)
12	KHASM EL GIRBA (k) (Atbara)	0.25	2780	STORAGE & ENERGY DAM (1.1)
48	SENNAR (s) (Blue Nile)	400	2300	STORAGE & ENERGY DAM (0.93)
49	ROSEIRES (r)	600	2300	STORAGE & ENERGY DAM (3.0)
(+4) 12	LAKE TANA (Blue Nile)	1000	NA	PLANNED STORAGE DAM (0.14)
(−15)	SUDD	1000	1860	JONGLEI PROJECT DRAINAGE
31	SOUTHERN SUDAN	900	1240	PROPOSED STORAGE ON THE UPPER WHITE NILE
13	BARO DAM (proposed) (Sobat) (b)			PROPOSED STORAGE (flood protection) (1.7)
(−3)	LAKE ALBERT	1400	1420	
21	OWEN FALLS (ow)	1400	1400	ENERGY & STORAGE (long term) (200)
(+7)	LAKE VICTORIA	1400	1400	
18	FLOW INTO LAKE VICTORIA			

Fig. 3.1 The Nile: Hydrological Regime and Storage

these losses, but it is still incomplete, partly because of the uncertainty concerning the environmental and social consequences, but mainly because of political unrest in the region.

The discharge of the White Nile out of the Sudd is at present, then, quite small, on average about 12 milliards per annum, but this is greatly increased by the large rivers running off the Ethiopian Highlands to the east. The Sobat, with Ethiopia's planned Baro Dam for flood protection and storage, adds an average of 12.9 milliards. The Blue Nile, on which a number of important storages have been constructed (notably the Sennar and Roseires Dams) or are planned in Sudan and Ethiopia, contributes the largest discharge of about 50 milliards per annum, and the Atbara adds another 12 milliards although this tributary can be dry in some seasons. As a result of these tributaries, the maximum discharge in the White Nile is achieved between Khartoum and Lake Nubia, with a distinct late summer maximum which becomes slightly later

downstream through Sudan and Egypt (Figure 3.1). The heaviest use of water is via the Aswan High Dam itself, discussed below, and, lower downstream, via a series of barrages largely used for diverting water for irrigation. This discharge at the dam is commonly quoted between 84 and 92 milliards per year, depending on whether the calendar year or hydrological year is used and depending on which period of years is averaged. The minimum discharge was in 1913/14 with only 42 milliards and the maximum in 1878/79 with 150 milliards. Table 3.2(b) gives some indication of the variability of flow in the main tributaries and Table 3.3 shows the full record of annual flows at Aswan from 1875 to 1987.

There has been considerable discussion about the reality of climatic change and its effect on rainfall totals and mean river discharges. Table 3.2 gives some indication that declining rainfall frequencies and totals have resulted in declining discharges in recent decades especially, but patterns are complicated by the fact that the Nile Basin transcends so many

Table 3.2 Rainfall and river flow changes in the Sudan

(a) Rainfall characteristics at Khartoum

Mean annual frequency of daily falls (mm)					Mean annual total (mm)
	1.0– 9.9	10.0– 19.9	20.0– 29.9	30.0– 39.9	40.0	
1920–39	11.2	3.1	1.45	1.10	0.95	209
1965–84	9.3	2.1	1.15	0.50	0.45	131
Percentage change	–17	–32	–21	–54	–53	–37

(b) Flow variability of the Nile river system in the Sudan

River and location	(i) Long-term mean annual flow (1912–73)	(ii) Standard deviation	(iii) Co-efficient of variation (%)	(iv) Mean annual flow (1961–73)	Percentage change (i)–(iv)
Bahr el Jebel at Mongalla	31.4	12.6	40.1	51.5	+64
White Nile at Malakal	29.4	5.7	19.4	36.8	+25
Blue Nile at Khartoum	50.4	10.3	20.4	38.5*	–22
Atbara at Nile confluence	11.9	3.9	32.8	8.4+	–29
Nile at Dougola	85.6	12.9	15.1	82.5	–11

*1965-73 at Roseires   + 1965-73

(Source: Shahin, 1985 and Walsh *et al.*, 1988)

climatic zones. Up to about 1978, droughts in Ethiopia with reduced flows in the Blue Nile have been more than compensated for by the abnormally high levels of Lake Victoria and hence higher discharges in the Bahr el Jebel (Upper White Nile) (see Table 3.2(b)). By 1978 there was a record level of water in Lake Nubia prompting fears of spillage and a new overflow was built. However, from 1980 onwards levels fell each year to only 3×10^9 m³ of water in July 1988 against the total capacity of about 110×10^9 m³. This would have been disastrous for Egypt without the highly publicized 'saving' floods of August 1988 which devastated Khartoum. Lake Victoria levels are now below average levels, so that the lower Nile is again dependent on the Blue Nile discharges. In the past, high Lake Victoria levels have helped cushion Egypt from the more severe influences of the Ethiopian drought, but this is no longer the case and a continuation of low Blue Nile discharges will have serious effects on Lake Nubia levels.

The pressure on the use of this precious resource is demonstrated in Table 3.4. The plans for the use of Nile waters by Burundi, Rwanda and Zaire are not available but are negligible; Tanzania and Kenya are unlikely to make large demands; and Uganda's use of water is still relatively small, despite the Owen Fall's Dam, though this situation may change. However, Egypt, Sudan and, to a lesser extent, Ethiopia have made and will make huge demands on the river. Apart from treaties made by colonial powers, notably between Britain, Egypt and Sudan in 1929, the first agreement between two independent countries was made by the 1959 'Nile Water Agreement' between Egypt and Sudan as a result of the planning of the Aswan High Dam. This agreement shared the discharge of the Nile, measured at Aswan, in the ratio of 3 to 1 in Egypt's favour and agreed an equal share in costs and benefits of future projects. Although Nile Basin surveys have taken place earlier this century, a major collaborative effort took place in 1967 when Kenya, Tanzania, Uganda, Sudan and Egypt agreed to start a hydrometeorological survey of the basins of Lakes Victoria, Kyoga and Albert. Also a 'Parliament of the Nile' was inaugurated in 1983, a product of a charter signed between Presidents Mubarak of Egypt and Nimeiri of Sudan, expressing the desire of both governments to be

Table 3.3 Hydrological year discharges at Aswan, 1875-1986 (10^9 m³)

Year	Volume	Year	Volume	Year	Volume	Year	Volume	Year	Volume	Year	Volume
1875/76	121	1895/96	122	1915/16	70	1935/36	94	1955/56	94	1975/76	110
1876/77	111	1896/97	122	1916/17	119	1936/37	85	1956/57	99	1976/77	84
1877/78	75	1897/98	92	1917/18	117	1937/38	81	1957/58	74	1977/78	91
1878/79	150	1898/99	118	1918/19	69	1938/39	104	1958/59	96	1978/79	85
1879/80	129	1899/1900	63	1919/20	77	1939/40	73	1959/60	98	1979/80	75
1880/81	99	1900/01	90	1920/21	80	1940/41	66	1960/61	81	1980/81	79
1881/82	97	1901/02	84	1921/22	75	1941/42	66	1961/62	107	1981/82	78
1882/83	99	1902/03	72	1922/23	88	1942/43	82	1962/63	90	1982/83	67
1883/84	111	1903/04	98	1923/24	88	1943/44	84	1963/64	94	1983/84	70
1884/85	98	1904/05	77	1924/25	84	1944/45	73	1964/65	128	1984/85	56
1885/86	97	1905/06	72	1925/26	69	1945/46	86	1965/66	88	1985/86	68
1886/87	102	1906/07	92	1926/27	84	1946/47	107	1966/67	80	1986/87	74
1887/88	115	1907/08	66	1927/28	73	1947/48	84	1967/68	98		
1888/89	74	1908/09	110	1928/29	84	1948/49	88	1968/69	74		
1889/90	99	1909/10	102	1929/30	98	1949/50	86	1969/70	74		
1890/91	118	1910/11	94	1930/31	68	1950/51	88	1970/71	92		
1891/92	108	1911/12	81	1931/32	80	1951/52	75	1971/72	90		
1892/93	131	1912/13	70	1932/33	88	1952/53	76	1972/73	65		
1893/94	109	1913/14	42	1933/34	84	1953/54	86	1973/74	90		
1894/95	133	1914/15	90	1934/35	95	1954/55	107	1974/75	97		

(Source: updated from Waterbury, 1979)

13

Table 3.4 Population and water demands of the nine countries sharing the Nile

Country (and year of Independence)	Percentage of total Nile Basin area*	Estimated total pop. (x 10⁶) 1981	Percentage of total Nile Basin pop. in 2000 +	Irrigated area 10³ hectares (future projection)	Ultimate water requirements (10⁹ m³)
Egypt (1923)	9.9	39.6	21.0	2770 (3400)	62.0
Sudan (1956)	62.7	17.0	10.3	1940 (2980)	23.8
Ethiopia (1880,1941)	12.3	29.7	17.7	40 (1930)	7.3
Uganda (1962)	7.8	12.8	7.8	3	1.5
Kenya (1963)	1.8	14.9	10.5	4	0.5
Tanzania (1961)	3.8	16.1	11.3	40	0.5
Burundi (1962)	0.1	4.0	2.3	n.a.	} 1.0
Rwanda (1962)	0.8	4.4	2.9	n.a.	
Zaire (1960)	0.8	27.8	16.2	n.a.	

* 3.03 (x 10⁶) km²   + taken as 240 x 10⁶   (Sources: Kashef, 1981; Mohamed, 1986)

permanently linked without losing their national identities. Much depends on political stability, especially in southern Sudan, and developments in Ethiopia, which is emerging as a potential major user of waters discharged out of the Ethiopian Highlands, now so important in sustaining discharges in the Lower Nile and levels in Lake Nubia.

From Table 3.4 and Figure 3.1, it can be seen that the ultimate estimated requirements of 62 milliards per year in Egypt is very close to the total discharge near Cairo, which makes Egypt very aware of upstream plans and of the possibilities of more efficient use of present resources. Much water which flows into the Mediterranean could be saved, but the maintenance of navigation levels for the cruise ships which travel between Luxor and Aswan in the winter tourist season remains of considerable value. Better use could be made of: the Nile Valley ground water resources, estimated at 220 milliards, of which only 1 milliard per year is used; unexploited Sinai reserves, estimated at 75 milliards; peak discharges and recycling schemes; benefits from future Sudanese schemes via the 50% share 1959 agreement; and more efficient use of the Aswan High Dam, the major scheme on the Nile.

The Aswan High Dam

The old Aswan Dam, constructed 1892–1902 with a storage capacity of one milliard and heightened in 1912 and 1934 to reach a maximum storage of 5.3 milliards, was largely used to control a network of irrigation drainage canals, but the rapid increases in population in both Sudan and Egypt led to further plans and the Aswan High project finally reached the drawing board by 1952. The finance derived from the World Bank plus Soviet engineering expertise, enabled President Nasser's prestige dam to be completed by 1967. It was sited 8 kilometres south of the old dam and its purpose was to provide long-term storage to meet the demands of agricultural expansion, to generate 10 billion kilowatts of electricity per year, to guarantee water supply during low flow years and to protect downstream areas from high floods. The dam is 4.2 km long and 163 m high, and its reservoir had a planned capacity of 164 milliards. However, after construction evaporation and seepage losses were greater than anticipated and maximum capacities achieved have been only about 115 milliards in 1975 and 1978. The dam is located in a site where possibly the highest insolation in the world could be expected, so that evaporation is very high (see Figure 3.1) and, as the lake increases in size, this becomes more significant. Also there are considerable seepage losses, which combine with evaporation losses to total 16 milliards

per year, instead of the 1–2 milliards per year estimated before construction. It seems that the effects of wind, increased surface area over shallow inlets and groundwater seepage were all underestimated, although it can be argued that seepage losses are in fact gains to groundwater reserves in the longer term.

It is also true that the potential of the dam for power generation has not been achieved. It has been suggested that 21% of the total flow by-passes the turbines and only 6.6 billion kW hours was being produced from the High Dam in 1976 out of the installed capacity of 10 billion kWh. To achieve this latter figure the dam has to be full and all turbines operating, but this has never been feasible. There are problems also with inadequate transmission capacity in lower Egypt and with optimizing agricultural and HEP uses, which are not always compatible. Nevertheless Aswan High Dam's HEP output plus the 2 billion kWh of the old Aswan power station make a massive contribution to Egypt's energy demands.

The total sediments in the river prior to dam construction have been estimated as 100–140 million tonnes per year, whilst sediment discharges below the dam recently amount to between 3 and 26 million tonnes per year. Evidently the difference is accumulating in the dam, an accumulation which will significantly reduce the dam's useful life. Much of the silt comes from the Ethiopian Highlands via the Blue Nile, where the two dams at Roseires and Sennar (Figure 3.1) should intercept much of it. However, these two dams meet 80% of Sudan's electricity demand each year and the sluice gates must be left open during the annual flood when the water is heavily silt-laden, otherwise the Roseires would be filled with sediment within four or five years. The silt is missed by much of Egyptian agriculture and the clearer water downstream from Aswan, with its high velocities, has a greater erosive capacity, but reports about the severity of these effects in the river channel itself vary from very serious to minima. What is agreed upon is the erosional effect in the Delta coastal area. The huge quantities of sediment once brought down to the Mediterranean, mainly via the channels near Rosetta (west) and Damietta (east), were then in reasonable balance with the erosive coastal processes, but now the rate of erosion is huge, 20–30 m per year at the Rosetta mouth, and the tourist industry has been affected over the entire Delta coast area including the resort of Alexandria. In addition, the question of the relative balance of fresh and salt water intrusion in the Delta area as a whole is serious in the context of the Delta's ecology.

Associated with sediment is the concentration of dissolved material in the river. The most severe effect is the trapping of nutrients for the once flourishing sardine industry whose catches in the Nile and the Mediterranean have dropped drastically. Although this is, in part, offset by a growing fishing industry in Lake Nubia, it is far from the main markets, is unlikely to recover losses and may suffer the same fate as a similar project in the Kariba dam where attempts to stock with fish failed miserably.

Other problems commonly referred to are those associated with irrigation. Perennial irrigation is now assured for many areas and cropped areas have increased from 3.9 million hectares in 1952 to more than 4.6 million hectares in 1977. The associated dangers of soil or water degradation through increased salinity have been alleviated by a pipe drainage scheme with further World Bank finance; and the fertilizing and leaching effects of the annual floods have been replaced by increased use of fertilizers. However, the spread of malaria and bilharzia (or schistosomiasis) diseases, especially in southern Egypt, is probably associated with the spread of perennial irrigation. Reduction of flushing floods has encouraged rodent populations to flourish and sewage systems to fester. Sanitation is at the heart of the huge bilharzia problem. The intended targets of land reclaimed from the desert are still far off and only about 190 000 hectares can be reasonably considered to have been reclaimed to date and much of this produces only relatively low yields.

Even in considering the many problems of the Aswan High Dam, one might still conclude that they do not detract from the huge contribution to Egypt's, and possibly Sudan's, economies. The dam saved lives by flood control in 1964, 1967 and 1975, it supplies about 58% of Egypt's energy; large areas of new land have been brought into production, and the benefits of a reliable water supply to Egypt's farmers are difficult to quantify.

Conclusion

The story of the Aswan High Dam can thus raise the question of whether the Third World is best served in developing its water resources via huge prestigious schemes which are often under considerable influence from outside powers. Some authors suggest that these accentuate regional disparities in welfare, as well as causing environmental problems, but this is surely to ignore the huge benefits they often bring. However, the scale of manipulation of the water in the hydrological cycle varies considerably from a single point (wells, shadufs, etc.), to a catchment scale, to a sub-regional scale or even to an international sub-continental scale. Clearly, the higher up this scale, the greater is the cost and the more sophisticated the organization and cooperation required. The inter-relationship between developments in water supply, with agriculture, industry, settlement and the environment has become obvious. In the developed world, the relationships between the water administrators, conservationists, industrialists, public consumers, agriculturalists, etc., are extremely complex. They have been developed over long periods of time and are still far from ideal. The developing countries will need time and money to proceed, yet they need the water now. It has been suggested by many, including the UN, that self-help schemes on modest scales, with an awareness of the inter-relatedness of activities with the environment, may prove the most successful starting points.

ASSIGNMENTS
---

1. Using the information in Table 3.1:
    (a) Calculate the percentage of precipitation which occurs as run-off for each continent and draw divided circles to illustrate information in the Table.
    (b) Comment on the availability of water in each continent.

2. From the details in Figure 3.1, produce a flow diagram to illustrate quantities of discharge throughout the Nile catchment. Use this diagram and information in Table 3.2(b), to explain patterns of flow.

3. Use the data in Table 3.3 to produce a graph of the '10-year running mean' of the Nile's annual run-off 1875–1987. Using this graph and the data in Table 3.2, consider to what extent there is clear evidence of a decline in the total water resources of the Nile Basin.

4. (a) List the benefits and problems resulting from the construction of the Aswan High Dam.
    (b) Find examples of other major reservoir schemes in the developing world and comment on some of their benefits and problems.

4 Soil Erosion in the Himalayas with Special Reference to Nepal

S J Kirkby and A Mellor

Introduction

The disastrous floods of 1988, affecting the Ganges–Brahamaputra delta in Bangladesh and Bengal state, India, have been linked in part with a whole series of environmental problems in the Himalayan region to the north. The sequence of events leading to river flooding is believed to commence with removal of the protective vegetation cover from the lower Himalayas and Siwalik Hills of Nepal and India. Good vegetation cover serves to minimize overland flow by intercepting a significant proportion of precipitation inputs to slopes and by ensuring high infiltration and moisture capacities of soils. Vegetation clearances lead to increased rates of overland flow which in turn may lead to accelerated rates of soil erosion (Figure 4.1). Consequently, affected catchments will experience both more rapidly rising floods and increased sediment load, with potentially disastrous consequences downstream. In other words, soil erosion is a problem in both the hills and the plains, and lies at the heart of Nepal's environmental and human crisis.

Geographical setting

Nepal occupies the central third of the Himalayan range and is located between India and the Chinese province of Tibet, between latitudes 27° and 30° N (Figure 4.2). Although these are sub-tropical latitudes, climate varies dramatically in response to a vast altitudinal range (50–8848 m above sea level). In Kathmandu (1324 m), mean monthly temperatures range from 9°C in January to 23°C in July, and the mean annual precipitation of 1000 mm is concentrated during the 100 days of the summer monsoon period between June and September.

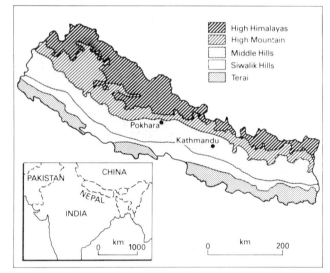

Fig. 4.2 Topographic Zones in Nepal

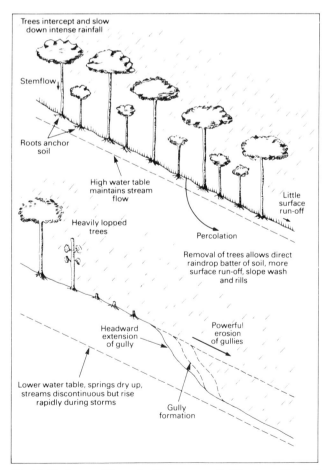

Fig. 4.1 The Impact of Vegetation Clearance upon Soil Erosion and Level of Water Table

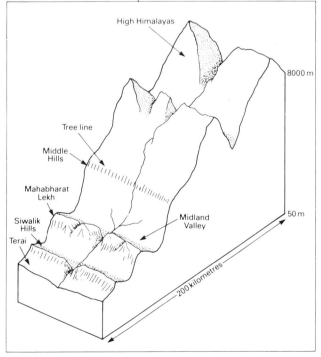

Fig. 4.3 Block Diagram of Topographic Zones

Nepal can be divided into four major topographic zones (Figures 4.2 and 4.3). The 'High Himalayan' zone consists of high mountains, glaciers, snowfields and alpine landscapes with a harsh climate, weakly developed soils and no agriculture. Rapid geomorphological processes ensure an enormous supply of sediment to rivers. The 'Middle Hill' zone, formerly forested, has better developed soils and intensive cultivation. It consists of steeply sloping hills up to about 4000 m in altitude and heavily farmed intra-montane basins (Figure 4.2). The 'Siwalik Hills' are formed of poorly consolidated sandstones and shales and are the most severely degraded of Nepalese environments. Finally, the 'Terai' zone is a very flat, low-lying area (below 160 m) and consists of recently deposited river sediments, forming the northern edge of the Ganges plain.

Causes of soil erosion

Soil erosion in Nepal reflects both natural and human influences. The landscapes of Nepal are naturally susceptible to erosion for a number of geological, geomorphological and climatic reasons. Geologically, the country is very young and tectonically active, much of the rapid uplift forming the Himalayas having occurred during the last 20 million years of Tertiary and Quaternary time. As a result of intense tectonic activity, most of Nepal is characterized by very high relief and steep, unstable slopes. These geological factors, in combination, render the country susceptible to mass movement in the form of land slides, debris flows and mud flows, all of which contribute to high river sediment yields. Nepal experiences a concentration of precipitation between June and September, with periods of heavy rain interspersed with a few days of dry weather. Rainfall of more than 100 mm per day is recorded somewhere in Nepal every year and 400 mm has been recorded in one day.

In addition to these natural factors, soil erosion can be accelerated by human activity. As 94% of Nepal's rapidly expanding population, currently at 17 million and growing at about 2.6% per year, is rural in character, demand for agricultural land increases. Consequently, peasant farmers, in particular, are being forced into increasingly marginal environments which are especially susceptible to soil erosion. Another significant cause of soil erosion is overgrazing of both forested and grassland areas.

Large areas in the Middle Hills of Nepal are being rapidly deforested, not only for agricultural purposes, but also for woodfuel and timber (Plate 4.1). Pessimists suggest that little timber will remain by the end of the century. As in many Third World countries, wood is the chief source of energy in Nepal. Demand for woodfuel exceeds natural replenishment rates in most of the hill areas and, in consequence, trees are excessively lopped, in many cases ultimately killing them and reducing the protection they offer to the soil. Deforestation, and thus soil erosion, spreads progressively outward from settlements. During the last twenty years the 'Chipko' movement has gathered support in Nepal and other parts of the Himalayas. Chipko means 'hug the trees' and refers to the action of women who protected trees from commercial logging by joining hands around the threatened trees.

Processes of soil erosion

Nepal displays a wide and complex range of topographic situations (Figure 4.3) and thus soil erosion takes on a variety of forms and occurs over a range of scales in the landscape. In

Plate 4.1 Deforestation in the Middle Hills of Nepal

many low-lying areas, however, soil deposition is more significant than erosion. This is particularly the case in parts of the Terai region and in intra-montane basins of the Middle Hill zone. The range of forms produced by soil erosion and deposition are illustrated in Figures 4.4, 4.5 and 4.6. In valley floor situations, lateral migration of rivers and streams frequently results in erosion of the low-level terraces. In spite of these problems, level valley floors below about 3500 m in altitude are almost invariably cultivated. Such sites are especially popular as they are easily irrigated for rice growing during the monsoon season. Furthermore, soils in valley bottoms are often fertile as they contain remnants of topsoil derived from upslope and/or upstream.

On hill slopes the Government's advisory limit of steepness for cultivation is 30° although many cultivated slopes are in excess of this, sometimes up to 50°. It is on such steep slopes that land slides, debris flows and mud flows occur most frequently. These mass movements, often lead to the destruction of agricultural land, property, communication networks and even to loss of life. On gentler slopes (30°), the erosion problem is still present though perhaps less dramatic. In areas with poor vegetation cover, soil material is initially detached by raindrop impact on the unprotected ground surface during monsoon storms, and is subsequently available for transport downslope. Such transport is normally most severe during periods of overland flow when soil material is moved by the process of sheetwash (Figure 4.5). Where there is considerable surface flow, rills may develop; these are small, closely spaced channels up to a few centimetres in depth. Rills indicate extremely high rates of soil erosion and if unchecked, may increase in size leading to gulley formation.

Gulleys are steep-sided valleys which carry water only after heavy rainfall. They may be tens of metres deep, almost vertically-sided and are linear features which yield extraordinarily large amounts of sediment. Unlike rills, gulleys cannot easily be controlled and often form permanent scars in the landscape. Movement of water downslope over a period of time results in the formation of small depressions at such

breaks. Subsequently, the depressions enlarge and coalesce to form a small channel. Erosion is concentrated at the upslope head of the gulleys where a near vertical scarp develops. Scouring at the base results in overdeepening of the channel and undermining of the headwall, which collapses and extends upslope (Figure 4.6). Consequently, gulley development occurs in an upslope direction.

Whereas soil erosion is a major problem in upland areas of Nepal, in the flat, low-lying Terai region, the problem is one of deposition rather than of erosion. Major tributaries of the River Ganges, such as the River Gandak, flow in a general N–S direction across the region. These tributaries enter the north of the region as large and complex braided systems but develop a more meandering character to the south. As these rivers are flowing over unconsolidated floodplain sediments, they are liable to change course rather rapidly during the monsoon season, particularly in the braided sections. Evidence for such

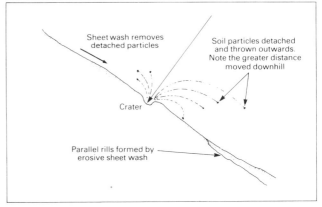

Fig. 4.5 Soil Erosion Mechanisms

changes exists in the form of meander cut offs, which occur where a meandering section of stream has been cut off by erosion, to provide a shorter course; sediment splays, which are large patches of sediment deposited on the surface of the floodplain during floods; and palaeochannels, which are abandoned sections of river channel. Traditionally, soil erosion is viewed as a physical process largely involving losses of soil in suspension. Such erosion is very evident in the landscape as seen by the range of landforms produced (Figure 4.4). Perhaps a more sinister form of soil erosion, however, is that of chemical losses in solution. Such losses go unseen in the landscape and are, therefore, not often accounted for. In upland areas of Nepal, the long term decline in soil nutrient status, if attributed solely to physical loss of soil, will be underestimated due to chemical losses. In contrast, the long-term decline in soil nutrient status in low-lying areas of Nepal may well be overestimated due not only to physical inputs from upslope but also due to chemical inputs. It might be possible to test this hypothesis by monitoring the chemical properties of the soil as well as their physical properties. Many studies of soil erosion base their interpretations solely on physical soil data.

Management of soil erosion

A Western-trained soil management specialist and a Nepalese farmer see soil erosion in very different ways. To the Western specialist the problem will be analysed in terms of the processes involved and will lead to the formulation of a plan centred on reduction of soil erosion. To the Nepalese peasant the main

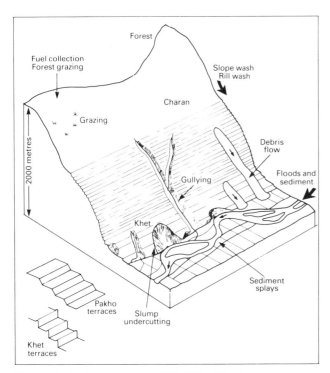

Fig. 4.4 Erosion Processes in the Middle Hills of Nepal

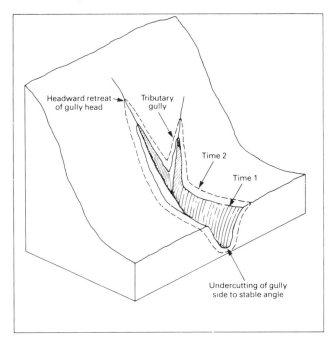

Fig. 4.6 Gulley Extension

problem is being able to produce a crop this year, thus avoiding starvation. Soil erosion is part of a much wider problem involving irrigation water, fertilizer and all the other elements of farming. Control of soil erosion is not an issue in itself, but part of the general land management plan. For instance, the Nepalese farmer has for thousands of years constructed terraces to facilitate irrigation, to reduce soil erosion and to increase crop yields; crop yields from terraced land are frequently double those from adjacent unterraced land. This indigenous management strategy, an example of 'ethnotechnology', has been tried and tested over generations and has proved to be largely successful. In contrast, many Western experts have concluded that much of the Middle Hills of Nepal cannot safely be farmed because the risk of erosion is unacceptably high. For the Nepalese farmer, the cost of the traditional farming system is paid in unending, back-breaking labour; many now find this unacceptable and are migrating to more easily farmed areas of the Terai lowlands.

As much of the landscape of Nepal is steeply sloping, one of the most common indigenous practices of soil conservation is that of terracing. Terracing serves to break the slope, thus reducing the effect of overland flow, and to create a series of level, cultivable surfaces upon which water can be retained. The resulting intricately stepped landscape is a characteristic of Nepal, particularly in the Middle Hills. Terraces are mostly earth-fronted, although stone-fronted examples can be seen. Often in combination with terracing, farmers construct diversion channels to direct water away from slopes which are particularly susceptible to erosion.

On the steeper slopes and at high altitudes, 'dry' terraces (*pakho*) predominate (Figure 4.4), the crops grown receiving no irrigation. Pakho terraces slope forwards, shedding water and sediment. Sediment yields of 20 tonnes per hectare have been recorded from such terraces. Although this value is rather high, it compares very favourably with values of over 200 tonnes per hectare from gulleys. In low-lying locations, farmers construct flat, irrigable terraces (*khet*) with rice as the major crop. Acceptable sediment yields of about 2 tonnes per hectare are recorded from *khet* terraces. It might seem sensible, therefore, to construct more *khet* terraces rather than *pakho* terraces. The time required to construct and maintain *khet*

terraces, however, is considerably greater than that required for *pakho* terraces. Furthermore, the soil eroded from *pakho* terraces is almost invariably intercepted by the *khet* terraces, thus adding to their fertility.

In order to reduce soil erosion, western experts suggested that *pakho* terraces should slope backwards into the hillside. When this was attempted, however, water saturated the soil causing debris and mudflows. Organic fertilizers such as crop residues, fire ashes, animal and human manure, and soils excavated from forests, are added liberally each year to both *khet* and *pakho* terraces to compensate for nutrient depletion through crop growth, physical soil loss and leaching. On a financial basis, these make more sense than the purchase of advanced chemical fertilizers since the average income in Nepal is no more than £100 per year. Soil quality is thus maintained and the effects of soil erosion are reduced.

Conclusion

Soil erosion has potentially devastating effects on the lives of the hill farmers of Nepal, since any reduction of productivity could lead to famine. Downstream, however, there are other problems; soil which has been eroded from the hills is deposited on the flood plains and destroys crops, or is deposited in the stream bed and causes flooding. In Bangladesh and along the Ganges in India, as population increases, people are forced to live in more hazardous locations near the rivers. Soil is also deposited in reservoirs, causing their storage capacity to be reduced, or the soil may silt up irrigation channels in the Terai and on the Ganges plain, thus threatening agricultural production on the crowded lowlands. High sediment loads in rivers also reduce the possibility of development of Hydro Electric Power (HEP) schemes.

Though this study has focused on the issue of soil erosion in Nepal, similar problems exist throughout the Himalayan regions of both India and Pakistan; indeed soil erosion is a problem throughout much of the sub-continent and threatens the sustainability of development. Many experts have suggested that reafforestation schemes could significantly reduce the amount of soil erosion. Local farmers too are well aware that maintenance of vegetation cover would protect their land. A number of such schemes have been started in different parts of the Himalayas, for example to the north of Pokhara, but there is, of course, a limit to the amount of land that can be taken out of farming in a crowded region where there is always the possibility of the monsoon rains failing and reducing food production.

ASSIGNMENTS
---

1. *Explain the main reasons for deforestation in Nepal.*
2. *Explain how deforestation in Nepal might lead to flooding in Bangladesh.*
3. *List the physical processes and resulting forms of soil erosion in Nepal.*
4. *What values of sediment yield have been recorded from the following Nepalese features?*
    (a) Pakho terraces
    (b) Khet terraces
    (c) Gulleys
5. *Discuss the suggestion that the traditional farming system in the Nepalese hills is the best response to the problem of soil erosion.*

5 Commercial Agriculture in the Third World: Problems and Prospects for Agriculture-dependent Countries

F Peck

Taking all developing countries together, the contribution of agriculture to GDP has fallen considerably in the last 20 years. In 1965 agriculture contributed 30% of GNP compared with only 19% in 1986. In spite of this average trend, agriculture continues to dominate the economy of many less developed countries (LDCs) in terms of production and export earnings. This chapter looks at some of the problems faced by these countries and illustrates some of the processes involved in a case study of Unilever's oil palm plantations in the Third World.

Agriculture-dependent countries in the Third World

Table 5.1 lists 27 LDCs where over 50% of merchandise exports consisted of agricultural commodities in 1986. In geographical terms, these countries form distinct clusters on a global scale. The countries of Burkina Faso, Mali, Ivory Coast and Ghana form one group in West Africa. Another major cluster consists of Ethiopia, Sudan, Somalia, The Central African Republic, Uganda, Kenya, Burundi, Rwanda, Tanzania

and Malawi in Eastern and Central Africa. Guatemala, El Salvador, Honduras, Nicaragua, Costa Rica, the Dominican Republic and Colombia form another grouping in Central America. The other countries include Burma (Myanma) and Thailand in South East Asia, Paraguay in South America, and the island countries of Madagascar, Mauritius and Sri Lanka in the Indian Ocean.

The African countries are particularly vulnerable. With the exception of the Ivory Coast, all the African countries listed have income levels (measured by Gross Domestic Product per head) well below the average for all LDCs. The African countries also have very high levels of dependence on agricultural production in terms of its contribution to GDP as well as to exports. In particular, Somalia, Uganda, Rwanda and Ethiopia rely almost exclusively on the production and export of agricultural commodities.

Most of these countries not only rely on agriculture in general, but also depend on a very narrow range of export crops, and in some cases, on one particular crop (Table 5.1). The production and export of coffee dominates 12 of these countries, especially Uganda, where coffee accounts for 93%

Table 5.1 LDCs dependent on agricultural commodities for over half of exports in 1988

| | GNP $ per capita | Role of agriculture | | | Population (millions) | Growth rates 1980–88 | |
		Percentage of GDP	Percentage of export	Main export (percentage of total)		Agriculture	Industry
Ethiopia	120	42	96	Coffee (62%)	47.4	−1.1	3.5
Burkina Faso	210	39	98	Cotton (51%)	8.5	6.4	3.7
Malawi	170	37	83	Tobacco (53%)	8.0	2.7	3.0
Mali	230	49	70	Cotton (42%)	8.0	0.3	8.1
Burma (Myanma)	200	48	86	Rice (42%)	40.0	4.7	6.3
Madagascar	190	41	70	Coffee (37%)	10.9	2.2	−1.0
Uganda	280	72	96	Coffee (93%)	16.2	0.3	6.4
Burundi	240	56	83	Coffee (87%)	5.1	3.1	5.8
Tanzania	160	66	75	Coffee (35%)	24.7	4.0	−2.0
Somalia	170	65	95	Bananas (11%)	5.9	3.9	2.3
CAR	380	44	60	Coffee (32%)	2.9	2.6	2.0
Rwanda	320	38	90	Coffee (68%)	6.7	0.3	3.6
Kenya	370	31	63	Coffee (26%)	22.4	3.3	2.8
Sudan	480	33	80	Cotton (39%)	23.8	2.7	3.6
Ghana	400	49	65	Cocoa (24%)	14.0	0.5	1.9
Sri Lanka	420	26	50	Tea (36%)	16.6	2.7	4.4
Dominican Rep.	720	23	53	Sugar (34%)	6.9	0.8	2.5
Ivory Coast	770	36	85	Cocoa (26%)	11.2	1.6	−2.4
Honduras	860	25	79	Bananas (31%)	4.8	1.1	0.8
Nicaragua	790	21	89	Coffee (27%)	3.6	−0.2	0.4
El Salvador	940	14	68	Coffee (59%)	5.0	−1.4	0.4
Guatemala	900	—	59	Coffee (31%)	8.7	−0.4	−3.0
Paraguay	1180	30	88	Cotton (34%)	4.0	2.7	0.1
Colombia	1180	19	49	Coffee (50%)	31.7	2.4	5.1
Costa Rica	1690	18	59	Bananas (27%)	2.7	2.5	2.3
All LDCs	**750**	**18**	**21**		**3952.0**	**3.7**	**5.3**

(Sources: *Commodity Trade and Price Trends*, 1987–88 edition, World Bank, Washington; *World Development Report, 1988*. World Bank, Washington)

of merchandise exports. Coffee is also the single most important cash crop in Ethiopia, The Central African Republic, Burundi, Tanzania, Rwanda and Kenya in Africa, as well as Nicaragua, El Salvador, Guatemala and Colombia in the Americas. Other countries have major exports of cotton (Burkina Faso, Mali, Sudan, Paraguay), tobacco (Malawi), tea (Sri Lanka), rice (Burma [Myanma], Thailand) cocoa (Ghana, Ivory Coast), bananas (Honduras, Costa Rica, Somalia) and sugar (Mauritius, Dominican Republic).

Another significant feature of many of these countries is that the growth rates in agriculture and industry tend to be lower than most other LDCs. Only four of the countries in Table 5.1 experienced growth rates in agriculture above the average for all LDCs between 1980 and 1986. Six countries actually experienced a net decline in agricultural production in these years. The performance of industry in these countries has been equally unimpressive. No less than nine countries actually experienced a net decline in industrial production, while only five countries expanded production faster than the average for all developing countries.

On all counts, it is the countries of Africa which appear to be in the most precarious position, since they are dependent on agricultural production and the export of one or two cash crops with no signs of industrialization. In short, it appears that these countries are becoming residualized. They are apparently unable to diversify their economies and are struggling to survive on an extremely vulnerable agricultural sector. The next section examines some of the consequences of this for these countries.

(a) The problem of competition

The vulnerability of these countries becomes clear when we examine the competitive nature of the world markets for the cash crops upon which they depend. Table 5.2 shows the most important cash crops exported from LDCs in 1982–84. Coffee and sugar are the most valuable commodities, followed by rubber, cotton, rice, cocoa, tobacco, tea, bananas and palm oil. These cash crops alone were worth over $34 000million

Table 5.2 Agricultural commodities in world trade (annual averages 1982–84)

Commodity	Total LDC exports ($mill.)	LDC share of total world exports (%)	Prominent LDC exporters (% LDC exports)
Coffee	9081	91	Brazil (21%) Colombia (16%)
Sugar	7947	74	Cuba (44%)
Rubber	3066	98	Malaysia (46%) Indonesia (26%)
Cotton	3033	46	Widespread
Rice	2191	57	Thailand (26%)
Cocoa	2070	91	Ivory Coast (27%) Ghana (14%) Brazil (11%)
Tobacco	2161	50	Widespread
Tea	1844	86	India (24%) Sri Lanka (20%)
Bananas	1241	86	Costa Rica (17%) Honduras (15%) Ecuador (12%)
Palm oil	1672	80	Malaysia (69%)

(Source: *Commodity Trade and Price Trends*, 1987–88 edition, World Bank, Washington)

annually in foreign earnings for the Third World in the mid-1980s, which is approximately 12% of the total value of all exports from LDCs (excluding oil). Producers of these commodities in LDCs are faced with a series of major problems which arise from the nature of these commodities.

1. Some of these crops are also cultivated in developed countries, hence LDCs have to compete with more intensive forms of agriculture. This is particularly true of tobacco and cotton, both of which are grown in the southern United States of America and northern Australia. Only 50% of world exports of tobacco and 46% of cotton originate in the Third World.

2. Many of these cash crops have natural substitutes. Sugar, for example, can be processed from sugar beet grown in the developed world instead of from sugar cane cultivated in the Caribbean. The EEC has increased its domestic sugar production since the early 1970s to become virtually self-sufficient, producing a surplus in the 1980s which is disposed of on world markets.

3. Several of these cash crops also have artificial substitutes. Most of the industrial crops have to compete with synthetic alternatives. Jute, sisal and rubber all have synthetic alternatives which have been developed by multinational companies seeking to control and improve the properties of materials used in production and also to protect themselves from price fluctuations which are characteristic of natural commodities from Third World countries.

The problems outlined above are shared by all developing countries involved in the export of agricultural commodities. For those countries which depend almost entirely upon these commodities, there is the added problem of competing with other more productive LDCs. Though there are many exceptions, as a rule LDCs experiencing manufacturing growth also have higher productivity in agriculture.

Most agriculture-dependent LDCs are not in a position to control global prices. Very few of those countries which rely on one or two cash crops for export earnings are prominent producers of such commodities in global terms. Uganda, for example, depends on coffee for 93% of its export earnings, but that country supplies only 3.5% of the world total exports. Rather, it is Brazil, an industrializing country, which contributes 21% of world exports of coffee and has powers to influence the price of coffee on the international market.

(b) The problem of price instability

The global markets for cash crops are not only highly competitive, for reasons outlined above, but they are also extremely volatile and subject to wide variations in prices from year to year. Variations in yield are one of the major causes of sharp fluctuations in prices for commodities. Producers in the Third World, therefore, cannot be sure from one year to the next how much income they will earn, and the governments of these countries face the prospect of sudden changes in export earnings.

In 1983–4, for instance, the quality of coffee production in Brazil was reduced through excessive rainfall, while production from the Ivory Coast was low because of drought. As a result, coffee prices increased sharply in the first quarter of 1984, benefiting East African countries such as Uganda and Burundi. Conversely, big increases in cotton production in China in 1985 depressed global prices for that commodity, adversely affecting smaller cotton exporters such as Burkina Faso and Mali in Africa and Paraguay in South America.

Recessions in the Developed World also cause sharp downturns in the income of agriculture-dependent countries in the Third World. Since 1980 the price of industrial crops like cotton and rubber has fallen to record low levels since the Second World War. Prices recovered in 1983, only to fall again in 1986.

Most food crops such as bananas, pineapples and coffee are also highly vulnerable to shifts in patterns of consumption and tastes in the Developed World. The production of tobacco is a clear example of a crop which is being threatened by changing life-styles in the Developed World. Also, shifts in drinking habits between coffee and tea have obvious implications for LDCs dependent on these crops. Food crop prices have, in fact, been under steady downward pressure in the mid-1980s due to a series of good harvests worldwide and poor growth of demand.

The incomes of producers in LDCs are also badly affected by the 'dumping' of surplus produce on world markets which forces prices down. Third World sugar producers, for example, have not only suffered from increased competition from sugar derived from sugar beet which effectively excludes them from the European market, but have also been affected by the variable size of the European surplus which adds to existing instabilities in the price of sugar on the global market.

The problem of dependency

Finally, many writers draw attention to the problem of 'dependency' in Third World development. This term describes conditions where development in LDCs is reliant upon resources and skills provided by developed countries. Since the break-up of formal colonial ties many large multinational companies (MNCs) have continued to exercise considerable control over the structure of marketing and production of cash crops in the Third World, a process which many authors describe as a form of 'neo-colonialism'. This means that countries which rely on the export of cash crops can still be highly dependent on the technical knowledge, skills and capital provided by Western MNCs. While MNCs are quick to point out that their activities do bring economic benefits to the countries in which they operate, the prime commercial concern of most MNCs is to guarantee an uninterrupted supply of agricultural commodities at minimal cost in order to ensure profitability in other parts of their organization. Conflicts of interest are therefore difficult to avoid.

Some MNCs maximize control of the whole chain of production and distribution by investing in land and plantation developments in Third World countries. The MNC also has direct control over production costs and pricing of commodities. This type of farming system has been criticized in the past on various grounds. The countries concerned have little control over the operations of these estates and a dependency on Western capital is sustained. In some countries, these estates also tend to occupy valuable farmland which could be used to grow food crops for the local population. The companies themselves, however, argue that they bring other benefits in terms of employment and infrastructure which would not otherwise have been developed. It is also the case that these companies share some of the financial risks associated with cultivation and are able to apply technologies to improve agricultural productivity.

Faced with the threat of confiscation of land and assets, many MNCs purchase commodities globally on an open market. Others may foster close relationships with a few key governments with whom they negotiate special terms for the supply of commodities. For the host countries this gives them some degree of control over agricultural development, although many are still dependent on inputs of technology and the purchasing strategies of MNCs. The bargaining power of producers, however, can be enhanced by the setting up of national government agencies and local growers' associations to negotiate with MNCs. This is the case in the Windward Islands in the Caribbean, where the British MNC Geest has developed a special trading relationship with growers associations to supply almost 65% of the total UK market for bananas.

These various strategies are likely to lead to quite different farming systems in Third World countries. Plantation systems tend to foster a duality in agriculture – a commercial monoculture using wage labour in some areas alongside a low productivity subsistence farming system which is often decanted to poorer land. In other situations, cash crops are incorporated into traditional farming rotations or produced in locally owned small plantations. The way in which MNCs decide to acquire inputs of commodities clearly influences local patterns of farming, ownership and control.

Global shift in oil palm production: the case of Unilever Plantation Group

In the previous section it was argued that agriculture-dependent LDCs have to face stiff international competition as well as cope with price instabilities and high levels of external control. This case study illustrates these problems with reference to the changing geography of palm oil production in the twentieth century. The main change has been the rapid decline of West Africa as a source of palm oil and a shift in production to South East Asia. The decisions made by major companies involved in plantation agriculture have played a significant role in determining this global shift. This can be illustrated by examining the changing geography of the plantation activities of Unilever, a British MNC which today operates oil palm estates in three continents.

Unilever's core business is in the production and distribution of food, drinks, detergents and personal products like soap, toothpaste and cosmetics, under familiar brand names such as Flora, Blue Band, Bird's Eye, Oxo, Lux, Vim, Persil and many others. The plantation interests of the company stem initially from its requirement for palm oil in the production of margarine and soaps. The oil palm operations are in Africa (Ghana, Zaire and formerly the Cameroons), South East Asia (Thailand and Malaysia) and the most recent developments in South America (Colombia) (Figure 5.1).

(a) Early developments in West Africa

Unilever interests in plantation agriculture date back to the early twentieth century when purchases of coconut groves were made in the Solomon Islands in the Pacific. In 1929, however, oil palm plantations were acquired in Nigeria and the Cameroons to ensure a steady supply of palm oil to factories in Europe manufacturing soaps.

West Africa was in many ways an obvious part of the world for such investment. The oil palm is native to West Africa. Indeed, during the nineteenth century the palms and kernels were drawn from trees growing naturally in the bush. There were early large scale oil palm plantations in some colonies, as in the French colony of Dahomy (modern Benin).

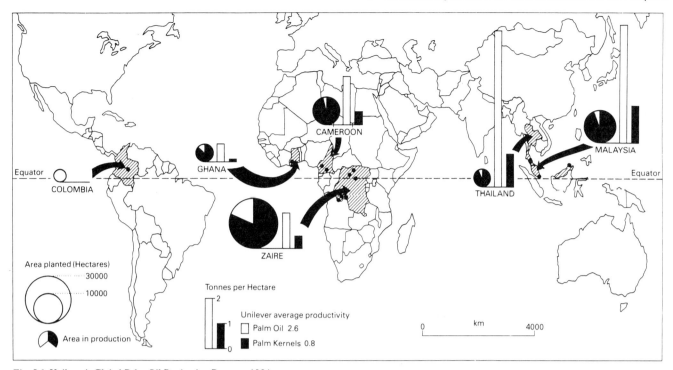

Fig. 5.1 Unilever's Global Palm Oil Production Patterns, 1984

Secondly, West Africa had well-established trade links with European countries, including the export of palm oil. In the nineteenth century, palm oil actually became the most important export from West Africa because of its use as a lubricant in many metal-processing industries in Europe. The infrastructure for production and marketing was therefore already well established.

(b) The shift to South East Asia
Political change in Africa in the 1950s and 1960s prompted a major shift in Unilever's oil palm activities world-wide. African countries were gaining independence from the colonial powers which placed Unilever's assets in danger. The new Republic of the Cameroon, for example, was set up in 1961 through the amalgamation of a former French colony (Cameroun) and the southern part of British Cameroon. Many of these new governments were antagonistic towards multinationals, especially those companies which owned large areas of farmland.

Unilever had already moved into the Far East in 1947 by acquiring a small oil palm plantation at Jahore in Malaysia. The political upheavals in Africa, however, prompted Unilever to develop an entirely new plantation in remote jungle in North Borneo, now the Saheb area of Malaysia. This new plantation began trading in 1960. Since that time Unilever's operations have consolidated in South East Asia, including the purchase of oil palm estates in Thailand and considerable investment in roads and housing.

As events unfolded, the transition to post-colonialism was accommodated in Unilever's two oil palm estates at N'dian and Lobe in the Cameroon which survived until the 1980s, managed mainly by Cameroonians. The comparative success of Unilever's operations in South East Asia, however, is clearly visible. Table 5.3 shows data on yields comparing the estates in Africa with those in other countries in 1984. Yields of palm oil in Unilever estates in Malaysia were 4.7 tonnes per hectare compared with only 1.9 tonnes per hectare in the Cameroons, 1.4 in Zaire and 0.7 in Ghana. Various factors may have

Table 5.3 Unilever's global palm oil production patterns, 1984

Country	Area planted (hectares)	Area in production (hectares)	Palm oil		Palm kernels	
			Production (tonnes)	Tonnes per hectare	Production (tonnes)	Tonnes per hectare
Africa	45 269	38 822	57 723	1.5	17 000	0.4
Ghana	3 925	3 432	2 500	0.7	500	0.1
Zaire	32 087	26 459	38 100	1.4	12 100	0.5
Cameroon	9 257	8 931	17 123	1.9	4 400	0.5
Asia	18 055	17 056	86 300	5.1	25 000	1.5
Malaysia	13 916	13 156	62 300	4.7	19 900	1.5
Thailand	4 139	3 900	24 000	6.2	5 100	1.3
S America	2 400	—	—	—	—	—
Colombia	2 400	—	—	—	—	—
TOTAL	**65 724**	**55 878**	**144 023**	**2.6**	**42 000**	**0.8**

(Source: Adapted from Unilever Plantations Group, *Technology Applied to Third World Needs*, External Affairs Department, London)

contributed to this contrast.

1. Environmental factors undoubtedly contribute to these differences in productivity. Tree diseases tend to be regionalized, and many African oil palm estates have suffered losses from a fungal disease known as Vascular Wilt which is still relatively uncommon in Malaysia.

2. Decisions made by Unilever, however, may also have contributed to these differences. The introduction of new breeds of disease-resistant trees and high-yielding oil palms has been concentrated in Malaysia. Another factor may be the tree planting operations of Unilever. Oil palms are thought to have a commercial life of about 25 years, hence the priority given to new development in Malaysia may have corresponded to a slow rate of tree replacement on African estates.

Table 5.4 Palm kernels and palm oil: price fluctuations 1970–1986

US$ per tonne – 1980 constant prices)		
Year	Kernels	Palm oil
1970	482	747
1971	395	711
1972	290	543
1973	557	814
1974	823	1184
1975	329	691
1976	361	638
1977	466	757
1978	452	746
1979	548	717
1980	345	584
1981	315	568
1982	267	449
1983	378	519
1984	556	768
1985	303	522
1986	125	267

(Source: *Commodity Trade and Price Trends*, 1987–88 edition, World Bank, Washington)

These weaknesses in Africa have been exposed by sharp fluctuations in palm oil prices in the 1980s (see Table 5.4). Palm oil producers have to compete with other sources of vegetable oil, in particular that extracted from soya beans. In 1986 oil palm prices were deflated by a series of good harvests of soya in the United States. The price of oil palm fell by virtually two-thirds between 1984 and 1986 to reach its lowest level since 1945.

The oil palm plantations in Africa were in a vulnerable position when prices fell, and as a consequence the operations in the Cameroons which dated back to 1929 were closed. In simple terms, the closure occurred because the operation could not trade profitably, but this inability to generate profit reflects a complex process of historical development and environmental change which dates back to the colonial period.

(c) The move into South America

The process is also on-going, as demonstrated by Unilever's move into South America in the 1980s. Oil palm estates have been developed in the Colombian Plains known as the Llanos and represent a major new departure for the company. It is intended that this venture will pioneer new techniques in clonal planting – cutting a piece of root from a highly successful plant and generating thousands of young palm trees from this

in a special nutrient medium developed by scientists in Colworth, England. Once the Colombian plantation is in production (there were 2400 hectares already planted but yet to reach production stage in 1984) the success of the venture could place question marks on other plantations in the Group.

Conclusion

The sequence of changes world-wide since the nineteenth century has been dramatic. Unilever account for only 2% of global oil palm production, but aggregate trade data clearly demonstrate that the spatial pattern of Unilever's development in the twentieth century is part of a much wider and more general trend in relocation of palm oil production. In the nineteenth century, palm oil production was dominated by West Africa. By the early 1980s, production of palm oil had shifted dramatically away from Africa towards South East Asia. Annual exports of palm oil from all developing countries in 1982–84 were valued at $1.672 million and ranked as the ninth most valuable export crop. Only 2% of these exports were from African countries while South East Asia accounted for 75%. Malaysia alone contributed 69% of these exports demonstrating the success of that country in adopting cash crops on a large-scale basis. It would appear that African countries have paid the price for this success.

It is difficult to be optimistic about the prospects of these agriculture-dependent LDCs. Indeed, for many, the perilous economic conditions are compounded by internal political struggles and civil war, while others are engaged in power struggles with neighbouring states. These conditions are unlikely to encourage sustained economic development. The fate of these countries appears still to rest on economic structures which were created in the colonial period and which have survived, in modified form, to the present time.

ASSIGNMENTS

---

1. *Using information in Table 5.2 construct a diagram to show the relative importance of different cash crops in exports from LDCs.*

2. *(a) Using information in Table 5.1, divide these agriculture-dependent countries into the following three groups:*
   (i) countries with over 80% of export earnings derived from agricultural commodities;
   (ii) countries with between 60 and 80% of export earnings derived from agricultural commodities;
   (iii) countries with between 40 and 60% of export earnings derived from agricultural commodities.
   (b) On a world outline, draw a map showing the distribution of these three groups of countries. Label on the map the chief export of each country.

3. *Calculate the proportion of the total LDC population accounted for by agriculture-dependent countries (Table 5.1, column 5).*

4. *Using the first half of the text, make a list of all the difficulties which agriculture-dependent countries may have to face. Write notes to show how these difficulties contributed to the closure of Unilever's oil palm operations in the Cameroons in 1984.*

6 Thailand and Burma (Myanma): Contrasts in Economic Development

M Sill

Introduction

Thailand and Burma (Myanma) are two countries in South East Asia which share a long common border (Figure 6.1). Each is focused on a broad rice-growing central plain, watered by the rivers Menam Chao Phraya and Irrawaddy respectively: teak-forested hills surround the river basins. In both countries a primate capital city, Bangkok and Rangoon, is located near the mouth of the central river. Each country, too, has a second city, Chiang Mai and Mandalay, located in a northern basin. These cities were both once capitals at the centre of earlier core regions of their respective states. In Burma (Myanma) and in Thailand today, the modern core region is centred on the present capital city which has developed from the nineteenth century as a port for the export of primary products and the import of manufactures, as both countries were drawn into trading relations with the Western world. Until 1948, Burma (Myanma) was part of the British Indian Empire: Thailand has never been formally colonized by a Western power, but from the middle of the nineteenth century was brought, by means of trading treaties, into the Western economic system. Until 1960, both countries were largely agricultural, exporting primary products such as rice, timber, rubber and gemstones. Industrial activity was restricted to simple agro-processing activities such as rice-milling and saw-milling of timber, as both countries imported most of their limited manufactured requirements.

Viewed from the late 1980s, however, Thailand and Burma (Myanma) contrast markedly in terms of economic structure and in stage of development. In brief, Thailand, through the rapid growth of an industrial sector, is, along with other Asian countries such as Malaysia and the Philippines, approaching the status of a newly industrializing country (NIC) following the development path of Pacific rim states such as South Korea, Taiwan, Hong Kong and Singapore. Burma (Myanma), on the other hand, has scarcely developed a manufacturing base; it is still a primary products producer and exporter, and, unlike Thailand, actively discourages tourism as a means of earning foreign exchange. With an average GNP per head in 1986 of only $200 US, Burma (Myanma) was the ninth poorest country in the world, classed by the World Bank as a low income economy and included in that sad group of least developed countries by the United Nations. And yet Burma (Myanma) once had large-scale rice exports; it has the world's finest teak resources in the Mount Pegu region; significant deposits of gemstones such as rubies, sapphires and fine quality jade, as well as major reserves of oil and gas surpassed, possibly, only by those of the Middle East. Thailand, with no greater resource base than Burma (Myanma), had an average GNP per head in 1988 of $1000 US, putting the country in the World Bank's lower-middle income bracket, still well behind NICs such as South Korea (with $3600 per head) but growing at a rapid rate. Reasons for this discrepancy in income will be considered later.

Contrasts in economic structures

In terms of overall economic structure, Table 6.1 shows that, in Thailand, manufacturing alone accounts for a greater share of GDP than agriculture, whilst in Burma (Myanma) primary production still dominates the domestic economy as the

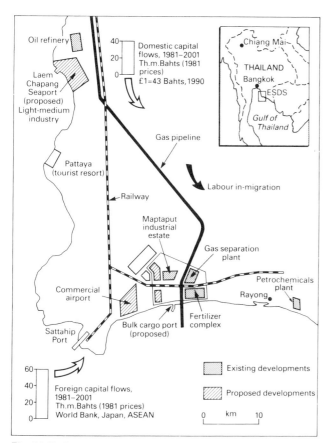

Fig. 6.1 Thailand: the Eastern Seaboard Development Scheme

Table 6.1 Thailand and Burma (Myanma): economic and employment structures 1986

	Thailand	Burma (Myanma)
Economic structure	**Percentage GDP**	**Percentage GDP**
Primary	16.7	48
Industry *	30.4	13
(Manufacturing)	(20.6)	(10.2)
Services	52.9	39
	100.0	100.0
Employment structure	**Percentage**	**Percentage**
Primary	65.0	65.3
Industry	16.4	11.1
(Manufacturing)	(9.0)	(8.7)
Services	18.6	23.6
	100.0	100.0

* Industry = Manufacturing + mining + utilities + construction

(Source: Economist Intelligence Unit, Thailand & Burma Country Profiles, 1987/88)

traditional pattern has changed little over the last thirty years. In Thailand, however, the shift of the factors of production into industry can be measured from the fact that in 1951 agriculture contributed 50% of GDP, industry 15% and manufacturing only 10%. In contrast, the employment structure of Thailand is still dominated by agriculture (Table 6.1), and as high a proportion of Thais are still employed on the land as in Burma (Myanma). Despite industrialization, the number of farmers increased in Thailand up to the early 1980s as the farming frontier was extended at the expense of forest, but with the recent closing of the land frontier this trend is likely to be reversed. Table 6.1 reveals a large productivity gap in agriculture, particularly in Thailand, where 65% of the employed population create scarcely 17% of the country's GDP. This reflects the inherently low productivity of Thai agriculture in which, for example, rice yields are low by Asian standards and have not increased significantly since the early 1970s. In contrast, Thai manufacturing accounts for over twice the share of GDP compared with the proportion of those employed in this sector. This reflects the capital-intensive nature of much Thai manufacturing, which has not yet begun to absorb rural labour on a large scale.

In terms of economic development, the major contrast between the two countries has been the evolution of a significant manufacturing base in Thailand since the early 1960s. This process can be summarised as a stage model. In stage I, which lasted up to the late 1950s, Thailand had only a small enclave manufacturing sector which was narrowly based on rice-milling and the processing of raw materials such as rubber and tin. Manufacturing served mainly export markets and, as is typical of enclave manufacturing, there were few backward economic linkages with the rest of the domestic economy. From the early 1960s, stage II can be identified, characterized by the widening of the manufacturing base through the development of import-substitution industries. The role of government was largely restricted to the provision of infrastructure such as roads and power generation and transmission facilities to support mainly private sector investment, both domestic and foreign, in industry. In this stage, the manufacture of largely non-durable consumer goods such as textiles, garments and leather goods became concentrated in the Greater Bangkok area. By the early 1970s Thailand had effectively reached a point where import-substitution, which by then had been extended to activities such as motor car assembly, had ceased to contribute to manufacturing growth and a choice of development routes was faced. Either Thailand could enter a stage III characterized by the domestically produced replacement of the import of consumer durable goods and intermediate products, a path followed by India and Brazil, or the export of manufactured goods could be expanded, as happened in Taiwan and South Korea. The evidence suggests that in stage III Thailand has followed the second export-oriented route. Exports of manufactured goods, principally to the USA, Japan, Singapore and the EEC, have grown rapidly since the early 1970s, from 5.5% of total exports by value in 1971 to 40% by 1985, when manufactured exports exceeded the value of traditional agricultural exports such as rice, rubber and tapioca, for the first time. Textiles and garments, benefiting from cheap, largely non-unionized labour, provided the initial engine of export growth, increasing from 0.8% to 8% of all exports by value between 1971 and 1982.

In recent years other manufactures such as electronics and

Table 6.2 Thailand: Structural change in the manufacturing sector 1951–1986

SECTOR	Percentages of total value-added		
	1951	1970	1986
Processed food, beverages & tobacco	50.4	41.5	29.7
Textiles, garments & leather	6.9	13.4	26.6
Wood and furniture	9.4	4.3	1.3
Minerals, metals & metal products	2.8	10.1	8.0
Transport equipment	6.9	5.8	7.8
Petroleum refining	0	7.5	3.9
Electrical machinery	0	1.4	2.0
Others	23.6	16.0	20.7
	100	100	100

(Sources: EIU Special Report No. 161, 1984; EIU Country Profile, 1987)

machinery and transport equipment have expanded more rapidly than textiles as the manufacturing base has widened. Table 6.2 shows the changes that have occurred since the early 1950s to the structure of Thailand's manufacturing sector. Although the processing of agricultural raw materials has declined relatively, if not absolutely, over this period, this sector is still the largest by value, reflecting the continued importance of agro-processing in the Thai economy. The decline in the wood and furniture sector probably reflects the rapid reduction of Thailand's formerly extensive forest resources, particularly teak, from 40% of the land area in 1960 to scarcely 20% by the late 1980s. In contrast, there has been a spectacular increase in the manufacture of textiles and clothing, whilst the making of electrical machinery (particularly integrated circuits), metal products and oil refining point to a widening manufacturing sector. Thailand, however, still has to develop a large-scale capital goods sector. There is no integrated iron and steel complex in the country; refined oil products, petrochemicals, machinery and transport equipment are still imported in considerable quantities. Stage IV, with a widely-based manufacturing profile typical of NICs has not yet been reached in Thailand, but may be by the mid-1990s.

In Burma (Myanma), unlike Thailand, neither the industrial sector in general, nor manufacturing in particular, has increased its share of GDP and, in fact, the sectoral breakdown of the economy has changed little since the 1930s. Indeed, agriculture has actually increased its contribution to the GDP from 35% in 1965 to 48% today, whilst that of industry has remained constant at about 13%. Manufacturing in Burma (Myanma) consists almost entirely of processing agricultural products such as rice and teak. Little surplus is produced for export and the undiversified nature of the Burmese economy is underlined by its pattern of exports which are dominated by three primary products. In 1986, rice, teak and pulses accounted for 86% of the value of Burma (Myanma)'s exports; minerals and gems contributed a further 8%. The more highly diversified Thai economy is reflected in Table 6.3 with the inclusion of manufactures and the wide range of other products which accounted for 44% of total exports. Furthermore, the open nature of the Thai economy stands in marked contrast to Burma (Myanma)'s self-imposed economic isolation. For example, Burma (Myanma)'s exports take a small, and declining, share of national GDP, decreasing from 4.8% to 4%

Table 6.3 Exports by commodity group: Thailand and Burma, 1986

Percentages of value			
Group	**Thailand**	**Group**	**Burma (Myanma)**
Chief agricultural products	32.6	Agricultural products	48.0
Textiles & garments	13.5	Forest products	41.1
Integrated circuits	5.0	Minerals & gems	8.0
Minerals & gems	3.5	Others	2.9
Tin	1.3		
Others (including other agricultural products)	44.1		100.0
	100.0		

(Source: EIU Country Profiles, 1987/88)

between 1981/2 and 1985/6. The figures for Thailand were much higher, at 20% and 21% respectively. Whilst Thailand's exports have increased rapidly in volume during the 1980s, those of Burma (Myanma) have actually declined. This decline continued through 1987, principally because of falling rice exports, the traditional backbone of Burma (Myanma)'s foreign trade. Recent increases in world rice prices make it difficult for Burma (Myanma) to compete with top-quality Thai rice because of the poor quality of the Burmese product caused by poor milling and storage facilities. Furthermore, as low-price, poor-quality Burmese rice tends to be exported to poor African countries, the recent decline in rice exports probably indicates the inability of Burma (Myanma)'s poorest trading partners to buy further imports.

The role of the state

Despite abundant natural and human resources, Burma (Myanma) remains under-developed and little changed since the early 1960s and the advent to power of General Ne Win. The economy is state planned and regulated, although the degree of state ownership is lower than would be found in a more fully socialist state. For example, small farms, transport undertakings and internal trade are predominantly in private hands, whilst manufacturing, mining, construction and financial and social services are owned and controlled by the state. Despite the low official income level of $200 per head, the extent of absolute poverty is small because of the general availability of cheap food and the workings of a large informal sector in the economy in the form of subsistence agriculture and black market activity, including large-scale smuggling across the Thai border, without which Rangoon would have very few consumer goods. Rather than emphasize economic transformation, much emphasis and investment has been directed towards social programmes such as health and education. For example, life expectancy in Burma (Myanma) increased from 44 to 60 years between 1960 and 1988; the infant mortality rate fell from 122 per 1000 live births in 1965 to 68 per 1000 in 1988; maternal mortality rates fell to 135 per 100 000 births in 1986 (Thailand 270 per 100 000 in 1986); in 1985, 97% of births in Burma (Myanma) were attended by health staff, compared with only 33% in Thailand. Furthermore, compared with Thailand, Burma (Myanma) has fewer people per physician (3740 compared with 6290), and a higher daily calorific supply (2609 calories compared with 2331) in 1988. The Burmese government has also made a great effort to increase the country's literacy rate, which is now at least 70% of the population.

In contrast to Burma (Myanma), which is an isolated and partially socialist state, Thailand has embarked on the vigorous pursuit of capitalist change. Great economic changes have occurred; economic growth rates have been more rapid than in Burma (Myanma), 7% per year since 1965 compared with 4%; manufacturing has expanded at an annual rate of 11% compared with sluggish growth in Burma (Myanma); export volumes have increased greatly (9% per year compared with a decline in Burma (Myanma) since 1965). And yet not all parts of Thailand have benefited from this economic change. Development has been very uneven spatially with most economic activity concentrated in the huge agglomeration of the Bangkok metropolitan area. Bangkok (population c. 6 millions) is highly primate, at least fifty times the size of the second city, Chiang Mai. Powerful economies of urban agglomeration exist in Bangkok so that most consumption goods industries as well as most of the import- and export-dependent manufacturing activities are located in the city, which is the country's dominant seaport, airport terminal, largest consumption market and financial and distribution centre. Table 6.4 shows that the Bangkok metropolis is the dominant manufacturing centre in Thailand, especially since much industrial activity recorded for the Centre Region, is located in districts close to the capital in the Greater Bangkok conurbation. Uneven spatial economic development has led to a serious maldistribution of income levels. The average per capita income in Bangkok in the early 1980s was over six times that in the poor, agricultural North East region, where almost 40% of the population lived, according to the World Bank, in absolute poverty. Figures such as these demonstrate the highly centralized process of accumulation and the uneven spatial distribution of the benefits of economic growth that have been a persistent feature of capitalist development in Thailand, as in other developing countries, over the last thirty years.

In recent years the Thai government has launched the Eastern Seaboard Development Scheme (ESDS) (Figure 6.1), aimed, in part, at offsetting the high degree of industrial concentration in the Bangkok metropolitan area. Other planning aims include the creation of a capital goods industrial base using indigenous materials such as natural gas, which has been extracted from the Gulf of Thailand over the last few years, and soda ash. The scheme is also designed to reduce Thailand's balance of payments deficit, caused mostly by the large-scale import of capital goods and machinery. To date, a petrochemicals complex making polyethylene, east of Rayong, was opened in 1982. A gas separation plant yielding methane, ethane, propane and butane, as well as some petrol, has recently been built with loans from the overseas Economic Cooperation Fund of Japan, and from the World Bank. This

Table 6.4 Thailand: Regional distribution of manufacturing, 1982

	Bangkok	Centre	North	North East	South	Total
Value added,%	51.7	36.0	4.0	4.6	3.7	100
Employment, %	35.3	30.2	10.0	12.3	12.2	100
Value added per employee, Bangkok=100	100	81	28	25	21	

(Source: World Bank Country Study, 1984)

plant provides the feedstock for an ethylene cracker on the Maptaput industrial estate (Figure 6.1), making ethylene and propylene: a second plant on the same site is being built with Japanese assistance, to make a range of petrochemicals used in the manufacture of foam, polyester and adhesives. Also on the Maptaput complex, a fertilizer plant producing urea and ammonia from local natural gas and potash is planned. As investment, both domestic and foreign, pours into new industrial capacity, the country's economy is shifting further away from its agricultural and agro-processing base. Yet those developments are capital-intensive and do little to employ Thailand's surplus rural labour. Concern has recently been expressed that the country should be aiming for a different type of industrialization, based on agricultural raw materials, using more labour-intensive methods and located in rural towns. In this way Thailand would become an NAC (newly agro-industrializing country), rather than an NIC. Perhaps Thailand needs movement in both directions.

Tourism and development

Within the service sectors of Burma (Myanma) and Thailand a major contrast can be identified with the respective contributions of tourism. In keeping with its policy of isolation from outside influences, Burma does not encourage tourism. A restricted number of visitor visas are issued for a maximum of seven days and tourists must enter the country by air through Rangoon airport. Since the attempted revolution of 1988, in which an estimated 3000 people were killed, tourism has effectively ceased to contribute to the economy, despite a considerable range of potential attractions, for example, wildlife, jungles and historic sites such as the magnificent Buddhist temple complex at Pagan. In sharp contrast, tourism has developed rapidly in Thailand over the last twenty years. More than thirty airlines fly into Bangkok airport and, since 1984, earnings from tourism have become the country's largest single source of foreign exchange. The number of foreign tourists increased from 1.5 million to over 4 million between 1979 and 1988, creating one full-time job in the tourist industry for every nine overseas visitors. As a tourist destination Thailand has several distinct attractions, such as beaches, tropical forests and nature reserves, competitively priced shopping and historic and cultural sites, such as the King's Palace in Bangkok. Because of its tropical climate, tourism is being promoted year-round, although in the summer monsoon months the number of visitors declines because of rain, humidity and lower sunshine hours.

Another attraction is the availability of sexual services: 70% of visitors are male, attracted, in some cases, to the red-light districts of Bangkok or to beach resorts such as Pattaya. Fortunately, this image is slowly changing. The Tourism Authority of Thailand is promoting the more wholesome resort of Phuket Island in the Andaman Sea, the island of Ko Samui in the Gulf of Thailand, the attractions of northern towns such as Chiang Mai and family resorts such as Hua Hin, · south of Bangkok. The Thais are also expanding into a wider range of leisure activities such as golf, targeted particularly at the Japanese. Golf courses are opening around Bangkok and golf package holidays are being promoted for Japanese, as well as for American and European holiday-makers.

Conclusion

To sum up, Burma (Myanma) and Thailand offer marked contrasts in terms of economic structure and stage of development. The former, in economic terms, represents the results of General Ne Win's, 'Burmese way to socialism', a mixture of Buddhism, international isolation and the state control of social, political and some economic activity. In consequence, changes to the country's economic structure have been minimal. Joint ventures with foreign firms are illegal, little private enterprise outside peasant farming is allowed, and visitors are not encouraged. The result has been economic stagnation, a large black market, an attempted revolution and the suspension of western foreign aid. And yet, despite this poor economic record, levels of health, nutrition and education are much higher than in most low-income countries, and are as high or higher than in richer Thailand. Thailand is in the process of transforming its economic structure through industrialization, in an attempt to emulate the East Asian NICs. This is, however, in spatial terms, a highly centralized process and the benefits of economic growth have so far been unevenly distributed, to the detriment of the population in the northern and north eastern peripheral regions, who are still largely dependent on low-productivity agriculture. Thailand is experiencing the growing pains of an emerging capitalist economy: Burma (Myanma) is consigned to a pre-industrial stage because of the imposition, since the early 1960s, of Ne Win's crippling brand of socialism.

ASSIGNMENTS
---

1. *With reference to the patterns of economic change in Thailand, consider the applicability of the following theories of economic development:*
   (a) the Myrdal model of cumulative causation;
   (b) Friedmann's centre–periphery model;
   (c) Rostow's theory of economic growth.

2. *'...Flying into Rangoon from Bangkok passengers are advised to put their watches back by 30 minutes, [but] time seems to have stood still in Burma for at least 40 years...' (The Economist, 30 July 1988)*
   Assess the validity of this statement.

7 The Growth of Manufacturing in the 'Newly Industrializing Countries' of the Third World

C S Morphet

Television manufacture in South East Asia

Rapid rates of industrialization

Among those countries which have been described as 'Third World' there is a small group which has undergone a startlingly rapid rate of industrialization in recent decades. From 1965 to 1980 the industrial market economies of the world together achieved an average annual growth in manufacturing output of just under 4%. For a handful of countries the same measure of growth averaged over 10%.

To maintain over a twenty-five year period an average annual rate of 10% is truly astounding. Table 7.1 identifies the countries with this record, and shows how a number of them have maintained relatively high rates of growth even into the 1980s when world trade declined and few developed countries managed to sustain growth rates of more than 1 or 2%.

In some of these countries the size of the manufacturing sector still remains small, and what we are witnessing is rapid growth from a small base. Libya, Botswana, Nigeria and Kenya have yet to reach the point where manufacturing makes a major contribution to their GDP. South Korea and Singapore, on the other hand, now have manufacturing sectors which are, relatively, as large as those of the developed countries of the world. A number of other countries in the same region of the world – Thailand, Indonesia, and Malaysia – are clearly also embarked on a sustained process of industrialization. Two other countries of South East Asia also demand our attention: the main source for Table 7.1 (the World Bank) does not present data for either Hong Kong or Taiwan, but evidence from other sources indicates a rapid and extensive growth in manufacturing output which compares with that of South Korea and Singapore. The four countries with this outstanding record have sometimes been referred to as the 'tigers' of South East Asia.

Table 7.1 Manufacturing growth: Countries with growth rates 10% per annum between 1965 and 1980.

Country	Growth rate 1965–1980	Growth rate 1980–1988	Manufacturing: share in GDP 1988
South Korea	18.7%	13.5%	32%
Nigeria	14.6%	−2.9%	18%
Libya	13.7%	n.a.	n.a.
Botswana	13.5%	5.0%	5%
Singapore	13.3%	4.8%	30%
Syria	12.2%	0.6%	n.a.
Taiwan*	12% (1974-84)	n.a.	36%
Indonesia	12%	13.1%	19%
Malaysia	11.1% (1970-81)	7.3%	n.a.
Thailand	10.9%	6.8%	24%
Kenya	10.5%	4.6%	12%
Hong Kong*	>10% 1967-82	n.a.	22%

* Data for Taiwan, Hong Kong from various sources – not strictly comparable.

(Source: World Bank)

Newly industrializing countries (NICs)

The term 'Newly industrializing countries' (NICs) has been applied to this group of nations. The term is sometimes applied to just the four 'tigers' of South East Asia and sometimes extended to include Brazil and Mexico, whose growth rates are marginally too low to be included in Table 7.1. It also sometimes includes the more recently industrialized countries of the European periphery, such as Greece and Portugal.

Much attention has focused, however, on the countries of South East Asia, where a more liberal application of the term NIC might extend to include Thailand, Indonesia and Malaysia as indicated above, and even perhaps the Philippines with a 7.5% growth in manufacturing between 1965 and 1980, and where manufacturing held a 25% share of GDP in 1988. Figure 7.1 is a map showing those countries of South East Asia whose recent rates of growth in manufacturing range from the considerable to the very rapid.

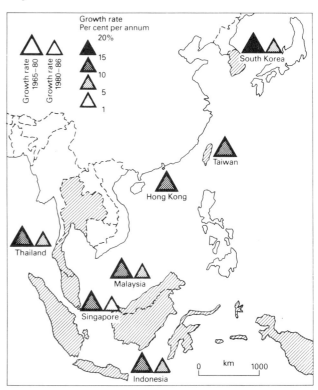

Fig. 7.1 South East Asia: Growth Rates in Manufacturing Industry, 1965–80 and 1980–86

NICs and the developing process

It is beyond the scope of this case study to try to account for this concentration of high rates of manufacturing growth in these countries of the Pacific Basin. Indeed the processes of growth in different countries with different cultures, different histories

29

and different factor endowments will of necessity vary. However, common elements in these growth processes can be identified. Growth has been based, certainly in the case of the four leading NICs, on an explicit policy of export-based manufacturing. This is to be contrasted with import-substituting manufacturing which would be designed to meet the demands of a home market probably protected from outside competition by a tariff barrier. The success of the export-based policy operated in, for example, Taiwan is shown by the fact that the country now exports goods and services to a value equivalent to around 60% of its GDP – exports of merchandise to the USA alone are equivalent to over 26% of GDP.

Secondly, the values and the political systems of these countries have something in common. The former includes the influence of Confucian philosophy on the region, a philosophy which stresses the virtue of hard work. It is also the case that throughout the region are to be found authoritarian governments of one sort or another – governments which are perhaps able to implement economic policies which produce short-term discomforts in pursuit of long-term gains, and certainly governments which while supporting a free-enterprise capitalist economy are highly interventionist in terms of their planning and promotion of industrial goals.

These are not, however, countries in which the mass of the people are blatantly exploited in pursuit of profits to be enjoyed by a small minority. Recent World Bank estimates suggest that in South Korea, for example, the richest 10% of households currently receive about 27% of the nation's household income. The corresponding figure for many developed countries is indeed lower than this, for the United Kingdom it is 23.4%, but for other developed countries (Italy, New Zealand, Australia, Sweden) it is a little higher and amongst the developing countries of the world it is usually very much higher indeed.

Other indicators illustrate the nature of the development process in these NICs: in the United Kingdom only 22% of the appropriate age group participated in further and higher education in 1987; in South Korea the corresponding fraction was 36%, in the Philippines 38% and in Thailand 20%.

Manufacturing industries in NICs: textiles, clothing and electronics

What is also evident is that in most cases, local raw materials have played a negligible direct role in the growth of manufacturing, although in a previously agricultural country like Taiwan the maintenance of a healthy agricultural sector has certainly played a part in supporting development. Nevertheless food processing declined as a proportion of manufacturing output in all of these Asian countries between 1965 and 1980. In South Korea it dropped from 26% to 16% of manufacturing output, in Taiwan it had declined to 12% by 1985, and while in Malaysia, Thailand and the Philippines food processing still accounts for a greater proportion of manufacturing output, its share is also in decline. In the city states of Hong Kong and Singapore food processing has of course never been so important. The countries have negligible agriculture and few natural resources of their own. It has been suggested that the only raw-material-based exports of Singapore (a country smaller than the Isle of Man) are goldfish and orchids!

There are two manufacturing sectors which are prominent in the economic growth of these NICs – the first is textiles and

clothing, the second electronics. The clothing industry is a classic labour-intensive manufacturing industry, and well placed to take advantage of the major resource available in the region – diligent and fairly low-paid labour. And yet in some of the leading NICs increasing competition (to some extent from elsewhere in Asia) combined with mounting protectionism in the industrialized world, have changed the nature of this industry too. In Taiwan, for example, the industry has recently declined in relative importance, and the industry has upgraded, changing away from low-cost small-scale labour-intensive production to production of higher quality (and thus higher profit) items with more advanced technology.

In 1983, electronics and electrical goods replaced textiles as Taiwan's largest export industry. This is an industry which began from nothing in the 1960s and has grown so fast that by 1978 Taiwan had become the world's largest producer of black-and-white television sets. Taiwan has gone on to become a major supplier of advanced colour sets to both US and European markets. This phenomenal transformation over a twenty-year period of a number of agricultural economies into leading suppliers of advanced electronics to world markets will be examined with particular reference to the growth of the television industry.

The growth of television production in the 'Third World'

Figure 7.2 shows how the source of imports of colour television sets into the UK, negligible in 1970, had grown to include Japan and Singapore as well as European countries by 1980, while by 1988 additional suppliers included Taiwan, Hong Kong, South Korea, Malaysia, Turkey and China. Other countries around the Third World produced black-and-white

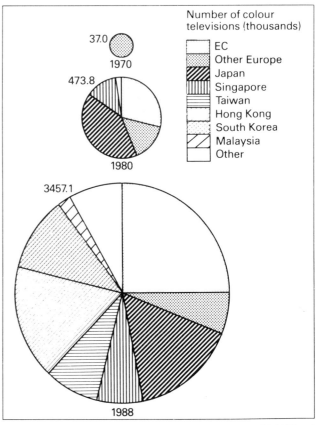

Fig. 7.2 Source of Imports of Colour Television Sets to UK, 1970, 1980, and 1988

televisions (or colour television sets for other than UK markets) and even by 1985 they included Tunisia, Mexico, Argentina and Brazil as well as Asian countries such as Indonesia, India, Pakistan, the Philippines, and Thailand.

The four leading NICs of South East Asia figure prominently as suppliers of sophisticated equipment. But as well as these four countries a number of other Far Eastern countries figure also as suppliers of consumer electronic equipment. It may appear rather puzzling that so many Third World countries have embarked on a programme of industrialization within which a high-technology industry such as television manufacture has played a role.

How then have countries such as Malaysia, Thailand, Indonesia and the Philippines, as well as the leading NICs, begun to export consumer electronics on to world markets?

Export platform investment – part of the story

The starting point for many of these Asian countries was a plentiful supply of cheap labour. But this of course is not enough; what is also necessary to make electronic goods is capital and 'know-how' technology. To some extent the necessary capital and technology was provided by American, European or Japanese companies who used Asia as an 'assembly platform', taking advantage of low wage rates and cheap modern transportation to ship in components, assemble them into electronic goods, and re-export the finished product to a market in the developed world.

Many developing countries encouraged this process by setting up 'Export Processing Zones' or 'Free Production Zones' in which multinational companies were encouraged to locate. Within such zones these companies were able to enjoy the advantages of cheap labour supplies with virtually no controls. They were often given tax concessions and also they were permitted to import components without any import duty or other restriction as long as the goods that they manufactured were for export. The working conditions established in these plants were much criticized in the West; it was claimed that a very high percentage of the workers were young females who were employed for their dexterity and in some cases virtually treated as disposable when the detailed assembly work ruined their eyesight.

A similar process of overseas assembly was followed by a variety of American and European television manufacturers. In Taiwan were soon to be found Philips, RCA, Grundig and Zenith; while in Singapore were Philips and Thomson-Brandt of France. Japanese multinationals were also involved in this export-platform assembly: Hitachi, Sanyo, Mitsubishi and Sony in Singapore; Sanyo and Sony in South Korea; Sanyo, Hitachi and Matsushita in Taiwan. The sets were then exported to the West and sold under their manufacturer's brand name. It soon became no surprise to see that a Philips television set had been manufactured in Singapore.

The development of indigenous companies

European or American firms manufacturing the newest products with the very latest technology are likely to manufacture in their home countries close to their research staff and their customers. Only at a much later stage in the life of a product will overseas manufacture, particularly 'export-platform' manufacture, become feasible. At an even further stage in the product life-cycle the technology of production

may become so routine that the technical skills of the multinationals afford them no advantage. It is at this stage that indigenous Third World companies may enter the market and manufacture successfully in competition with the multinationals.

It can be argued that the production of radio sets reached this point a long time ago, that the production of black-and-white television sets reached this point around a decade ago, and the production of colour television sets has hovered around this point for a number of years. Continued product innovation (Teletext; FST technology) retains a slender advantage for the major manufacturers.

This 'maturing' of the product technology has had evident implications for the location of television manufacturing, particularly since television manufacture is essentially an assembly process. All the parts can be bought in – the tube, the transistors and capacitors, and so on – and the process of manufacture or assembly may consist only of fitting together these parts, parts which may have been acquired from a technically advanced supplier in Japan or the USA, and which therefore incorporate the high technology within them. As the television industry has developed, this has become increasingly the case, indeed with modern microcircuits the amount of electronic assembly is reduced even further – a tuner need no longer be assembled from discrete electronic components like

Table 7.2 The increased diversity of suppliers

Market shares in British colour TV market (percentages)		
	1980	1986
Ferguson	25	12
Philips/Pye	25	12
Hitachi	10	7
Toshiba	10	6
Sony	7	3–4
ITT	7	3–4
Panasonic	5	3–4
Other	11	52

(Source: *Market Intelligence*, December 1987)

transistors, the whole thing can be bought on a 'chip'.

As the technology has matured, indigenous companies in the Far East have been able to enter television production. What many such companies have lacked is the ability to market their sets in the West. It is here that the major retailing groups of Europe and America have played a part. In America retail chains such as Sears and JC Penney have marketed under their own brand names sets produced in South Korea. In Britain, the leading chain Dixons maintains offices in Hong Kong, Japan and Singapore and distributes sets throughout the Far East to market under its own label Saisho or the label Matsui, that of its subsidiary Currys.

The rapidly increasing number of colour television sets produced and marketed in Britain by other than the major manufacturers is evident from Table 7.2, and equally evident from the shop window of any high-street television retailer.

NIC giants in the electronics industry

While some of the indigenous television manufacturers in the NICs may indeed be relatively small companies selling their products in the UK, there are some extraordinary exceptions. Despite what might be held to be the immensely powerful

31

position of the multinational companies, a number of indigenous companies, particularly in South Korea and to a lesser extent in Taiwan, have come to challenge and even surpass the established consumer electronics groups of Japan and the West. In South Korea there are Samsung and Goldstar (and to a lesser extent Daewoo) while in Taiwan there is Tatung. The rise of these companies has not been widely considered in Western accounts of the electronics industry, and their histories deserve to be better understood.

Goldstar is part of the Korean 'Lucky Group' a vast conglomerate with origins as a trading company. It began in electronics some thirty years ago manufacturing radio valves and now it realistically aspires to become one of the world's top ten electronics companies by the early 1990s. Goldstar began consumer electronics manufacture by buying most of its electronic components from Japan, and its television sets were sold under retailers' brand names in the USA. Even in the mid-1980s Goldstar was still reliant on Japan for electronic components, a situation made unacceptable by the strong yen as well as by the stated reluctance of Japanese manufacturers to trade in the most up-to-date technology. So now Goldstar has begun to manufacture semiconductors.

Even bigger than Goldstar is Samsung of South Korea whose semiconductor manufacturing began in 1985 in what is now one of the largest such plants in the world. Samsung is competing in a capital- and technology-intensive business where low-cost labour offers it absolutely no advantages over US and Japanese rivals. No longer can South Korea be seen as a country whose industrial development relies on low wages.

But such large-scale indigenous developments have not taken place in the other countries of South East Asia. Thus, as well as having much in common, the fast growing economies of the region also have many differences. Singapore's electronics industry is dominated by multinational firms, reflecting the policy of welcoming foreign direct investment almost without reservation. Hong Kong has fewer multi-nationals but, unlike Taiwan and South Korea, has not developed large indigenous corporations. These differences require local explanations and remind us that any account which treated the countries of South East Asia as undifferentiated sources of cheap labour would be severely deficient.

Export platform investment moves on

The multinational activity in the four original NICs is to some extent a victim of its own success, for wage rates have risen, and thus the costs of assembling low-technology electronic goods in these countries have begun to threaten profits. The reaction of these multinationals can be illustrated by the case of Sony of Japan. Until recently only 25% of Sony's production took place outside Japan, and most of that was in its long-established factories in the US and Western Europe. It has been the impact of the rising yen that has obliged Sony to look to low-cost production sites in South East Asia, where the company is now building four new plants, one in Singapore, two in Malaysia and one in Thailand. In accordance with Singapore's status as an NIC the plant located there will serve as Sony's engineering centre for the Asian region outside Japan. In Malaysia one plant will manufacture colour TVs and TV components and the other will manufacture audio equipment, while in Thailand the product will be video cassette tapes. In accordance with the accepted ideas of 'export platform

investment' the factory in Bangkok will pay the statutory minimum wage ((US)$ 2.90 a day), and Sony has been granted a three-year tax holiday by the Thai government.

... and back home again?

Cheap labour is not the only consideration in the location of production for television manufacture. If it were, production in countries such as the UK, West Germany and the USA would no longer exist. Moreover we would not be seeing investment in the UK by Japanese (and even by Taiwanese) electronics companies. Sony began manufacturing at Bridgend in Wales in 1974. Other firms followed, Matsushita (National Panasonic) in 1975, Mitsubishi in 1979, Sanyo in 1981, Hitachi in 1979 and Toshiba in 1978. The Taiwanese electronics giant Tatung acquired a factory at Bridgnorth from the Decca company in the late 1970s. What has made this possible is increased automation and the reduced demand for labour which results. In some cases automated assembly in the West will be cheaper than manual assembly in the Far East. Another important reason for continued investment in the West is the existence of tariff and other import barriers in both the US and Europe. Firms hoping to serve European markets may well search out a manufacturing site within the European Community, and expect to market their goods without restraint in the 'single European Market' of 1992.

It remains to be seen whether the NICs will continue to adapt if their low-wage advantages are annulled by these sorts of technical developments and if their products are subject to more and more import restrictions by countries of the industrialized world who increasingly fear for their own industrial health. The route now being followed by South Korea and Taiwan, who are concerned to produce a highly educated workforce while continuing to move into higher and higher technology products, leads some commentators to suggest that the path which Japan pioneered a decade or two earlier is about to be followed by the leading NICs. Although Taiwan continues to offer inducements to attract foreign investment, all projects must be approved by the Ministry of Economic Affairs, and investments in the light-manufacturing sector are discouraged unless they introduce new technologies, new markets, or are located in the periphery of the country. Capital-intensive and high-technology investments are, however, welcome. Just as 'Made in Japan' is now accepted in the West as a mark of quality, so might 'Made in Taiwan' be similarly accepted in the very near future, perhaps leaving developing countries of South East Asia such as Thailand and Malaysia to fill the role in the global manufacturing system which the leading NICs now occupy.

| ASSIGNMENTS |

1. *Conduct a survey of the country of origin of television sets on sale in a large retail store. Find out which manufacturers produce sets in which countries, and compare your results with Figure 7.2 and Table 7.1. Comment on any changes that have occurred since these data were compiled.*

2. *What is meant by the term 'assembly platform'? What evidence can be found in this case study to challenge the orthodox view that manufacturing development in the Third World is predominantly an 'export platform' activity dominated by multinational companies?*

8 Urbanization Trends in Africa

J C Sowden

Introduction

Any assessment of urbanization in Africa is fraught with difficulties largely because of problems of definition and data availability. The designation of what is 'urban' depends on the individual historical, political, cultural and administrative circumstances of a country. The data problems arise from the absence of regular and reliable censuses in many countries, the fact that many urban residents are temporary migrants, and the currently very rapid rates of urban growth. Furthermore, considerable diversity exists within Africa. This applies to all aspects of its physical and human geography, and not least to its urban centres. Cities often reflect the culture of the region in which they have grown, so one can refer to the 'North American city' or the 'Chinese city' as having certain characteristics which make them different from cities elsewhere. Africa is too big a continent with too varied a history to allow such generalizations. But it is possible to identify three broad cultural and historical traditions in Africa which are reflected in the present urban geography. This 'triple heritage' comprises indigenous African, Muslim/Arab and European/Christian influences, and the interplay between them gives identity to different parts of the continent and is reflected in the forms of urban development. Figure 8.1 shows the urban geography of the continent as it had emerged by the middle of the eighteenth century.

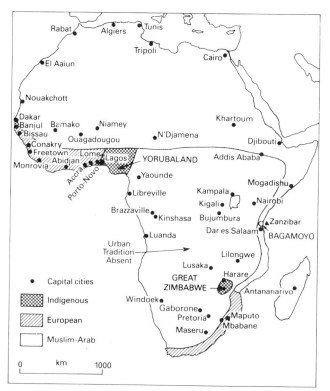

Fig. 8.1 Africa's Triple Heritage of Urbanization and Capital Cities, 1990

Pre-colonial Africa

The major influence in this period was Islam. The religion was brought by Arab invasions into North Africa shortly after the death of Muhammad in 632 and spread rapidly westward to the Maghreb. Urban life had existed in this part of Africa in the Ancient World of the Pharaohs, Phoenicians, Greeks and Romans, but it was the Arabs who laid the basis for towns which have survived to the present. Cairo, founded in 970, is now the largest city in Africa. Arab traders established routes across the Sahara to the Sudanic trading centres of the Sahel where towns such as Timbuctu had arisen. The main area of Arab urban influence south of the Sahara was along the East African coast. Here, a string of coastal trading settlements extended from Mogadishu to as far south as Sofala. Most of these early Arab towns were in place by the fourteenth century.

Apart from the towns in the interior of West Africa, there were few indigenous towns elsewhere, although the stone ruins of Great Zimbabwe suggest an urban type of economy.

From the sixteenth century onwards, various European nations began to establish trading posts around the African coast, mainly in southern Africa and West Africa.

The colonial period

The 'Scramble for Africa' which increased in intensity after 1850 has been described as a division of Africa by Europeans for Europeans. At the Berlin Conference of 1885 the major European powers agreed certain 'rules' for carving up the continent amongst themselves. Chief among these was the idea of 'spheres of influence' which explains the shape and size of the present states and the location of their capital cities. Under the rules of the 'scramble', a would-be colonizer had first to establish its control along a stretch of coastline, and from there it could extend its 'influence' inland. In West Africa the stretches of coast were short with many trading posts close together like beads on a string. The coastline of modern Gambia is only 50 kilometres wide, Togo is 75 kilometres and Benin 100 kilometres.

Colonialism brought new kinds of towns, with more specialized functions. Administrative centres arose to govern the colonial territories; these were often located on the coast where they could be linked by sea to the metropolitan power in Europe. Ports were needed to handle imperial trade. In many cases the function of port and administrative centre were combined in the same settlement – Freetown, Lagos and Dar es Salaam are examples. Centres to serve areas of European settlement grew up in highland areas, for example, Nairobi and Harare. Many mining towns appeared as minerals were discovered – for example, Johannesburg and Lubumbashi.

These towns were planned with a distinctive morphology which separated the colonial administrative and residential areas from the indigenous 'African' quarter. The pace of urban growth during the colonial period was controlled by the authorities and was relatively slow.

The colonial period had a major effect on the urban geography of the continent, and explains why so many capital cities are ports (see Figure 8.2). Only nine coastal states do not have port capitals, and of these most have capitals that pre-date the colonial period – Cairo, Addis Ababa, Khartoum.

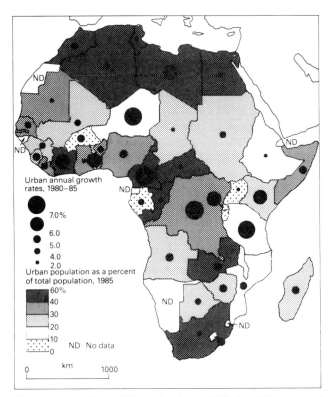

Fig. 8.2 Growth Rates of Urban Population, 1980–85 and Proportion of Urban Dwellers, 1985

Contemporary urban development

With approximately 30% of its population as urban dwellers, Africa is the least urbanized region in the developing world, yet its cities are among the most rapidly growing. Between 1980 and 1985, of the 42 African countries with populations above one million people, nine had urban growth rates above 6% per annum (Figure 8.2). Although this reveals a decrease from the rates of growth experienced between 1965 and 1980, when twenty-three countries showed rates in excess of 6%, the pace of urban growth in Africa is still rapid. The average for all developing countries between 1980 and 1985 was 3.8% and for most West European countries it was 1.5%. The slow-down in growth is particularly marked in Mauretania, Libya, Chad, Guinea, Benin, Ethiopia, Kenya, Mozambique, Zambia and Zimbabwe. Twelve countries showed an increase in the rate of urban growth, but it was less than two percentage points. These countries were Egypt, Niger, Burkina Faso, Sierra Leone, Ghana, Nigeria, Gabon, Congo, Zaire, Rwanda, Burundi, and the Republic of South Africa. So while there has been some slowing in urban growth rates, it is not evenly spread throughout the continent, and African cities are still growing faster than the average for all developing countries.

Although Africa as a whole is much less urbanized than other developing regions, there is considerable diversity between countries (Figure 8.2). The long urban tradition of the countries of the Arab world in North Africa can be clearly

seen. The high rate of urbanization of South Africa and Zambia reflects particular circumstances such as European settlement or the development of mining which has led to the growth of specialized towns. The low levels of urbanization found in the broad band of countries which extend through the Sahel and much of eastern Africa is linked to the limited penetration of such areas in the colonial era and the contemporary dominant position of agriculture in the economies of these countries. There is a broadly inverse relationship between the percentage of the population living in towns and the percentage of the labour force engaged in agriculture.

Migration and urban growth

The popular image of urban growth in most Third World countries is that it is fuelled by massive rural-to-urban migration. Whilst migration is particularly important in the early stages of rapid urban growth, meaning that a very large proportion of the population were born elsewhere, over time its contribution tends to diminish and that of natural increase to grow. The initially high rates of migration reflect both lack of opportunity in rural areas and the perceived advantages of urban life. In Sub-Saharan Africa only 10% of the rural population have access to a safe water supply, compared with over 60% in urban areas. However, in many African cities the permanency of migration can be as important as its volume. Most African migrants retain contact with their rural background and, in the past, many have tended to return there. In the Sahel, seasonal movement into towns is still a feature and in central Africa 'circular' migration of young men leaving their families for part of the year or a few years is still common. Over all, whilst length of stay is probably increasing, the African migrant to an urban area is still less committed to the urban way of life than in any other part of the Third World. Most migrants are in the 16 to 45 age group and the majority still tend to be men.

For example, males increased by 290 000 in Nairobi (1962–1979) and females by only 225 000. However, there is evidence that this is now changing. In East Africa the pattern is for married men to move to town on their own, to be followed by their wives once employment and accommodation has been found. What is clear is that, formerly, few women migrated to urban areas independently of men, largely because of the limited job opportunities for them and the traditional roles they are expected to play. However, even this is beginning to change and studies in Lesotho, Kampala and Dar es Salaam have noted some increase in independent female migrants to urban areas. The number of females per 1000 males in Dar es Salaam increased from 815 in 1967 to 865 in 1978 and 901 in 1988, an indication of the trend of change but also of the continuing dominance of males.

Consequences of rapid urban growth

During the past decade most African countries have experienced slow economic growth largely because the commodities which form the mainstay of their exports have been affected by low prices in world markets. This has slowed down the rate at which new jobs can be created, especially in the urban labour market, and has led to urban under-employment and unemployment. In these circumstances many people find employment in the informal sector as domestic servants, street hawkers, casual labourers, craftworkers and so on. According to some economists the informal sector is inefficient and has low levels of productivity and wages. But others challenge this view and argue that, although wages are low, they are no lower than they are in the formal sector. Urban poverty is something that affects most urban dwellers and is not confined to the informal sector.

Other consequences of rapid urban growth are over-crowding and inadequate access to services. There is no way in which urban authorities can provide housing for the rapidly growing populations of African cities. At best they can survey sites and provide a rudimentary water supply. The majority of urban dwellers in Africa live in informal squatter settlements with unpaved roads, few basic services and houses of semi-permanent materials, usually with mud and wattle walls and a grass roof. About 60% of the urban population of Africa lives in squatter settlements, compared with 20–30% in Asia and Latin America. The experience of Latin America is that, given time, these squatter settlements show improvement in the quality of the buildings and in their access to basic services which has led to their being called 'slums of hope'. The situation in Africa is not so clear because the rate of urban growth is more rapid and more recent, and the extent of poverty is greater. Consequently conditions in some squatter settlements such as Nairobi's Mathare Valley are very bad.

In spite of all these negative effects cities make a positive contribution to the economic life of their country. For example, Nairobi, which contains 5.2% of Kenya's population, contributes 20% of the country's national income.

Policy responses to rapid urbanization

It is only recently that the positive aspects of cities have been appreciated by some governments. During the 1960s and 1970s several African countries adopted a series of measures to try to curb or re-direct urban growth. This was a time when several countries, having recently achieved independence, were attempting to create a 'new geography of development' which met their own needs more efficiently than the inherited colonial spatial framework. This had been export-orientated and it was believed that this had given undue prominence to the capital city. The national plans for both Tanzania (1969) and Kenya (1970) contained proposals to spread development to nine selected towns throughout their respective countries to curb further growth in Dar es Salaam and Nairobi. These proposals were not accompanied by concrete plans specifying how the policies were to be implemented, and both came to nothing.

Some countries have adopted more radical ideas and propose to create new capitals away from existing centres of administration. These include Ivory Coast (at Yamoussoukro), Nigeria (at Abuja), and Tanzania (at Dodoma). Such ventures are extremely costly, and while governments have control over their own departments, they may not be able to persuade commercial and industrial organizations to follow them. Thus the pull of the existing centres remains.

Although some countries still pin their hopes on the kinds of spatial policies just outlined, most now realize that rapid urban growth is a fact of life. The problem is to accommodate it and to minimize its most harmful effects. The most recent World Bank urban aid programmes concentrate on improving urban management rather than the physical infrastructure of cities in an attempt to help countries to solve these problems for themselves.

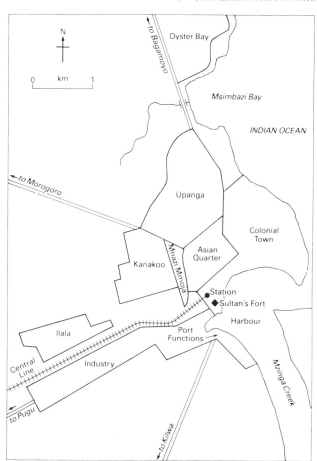

Fig. 8.3 Structure of Dar es Salaam, about 1960

Case study – Dar es Salaam

In this final section we will examine briefly some of the features of Dar es Salaam, the capital of Tanzania, to illustrate the general points made earlier.

The coast of East Africa has a long history of urbanization, going back to the tenth century. However, Dar es Salaam was not one of the early Arab settlements. The main port on this part of the coast was Bagamoyo which is 50 kilometres north of Dar es Salaam (Figure 8.1). Many European expeditions to the interior left from Bagamoyo, including that of Stanley in 1871, in his search for Dr Livingstone. The advantages of Dar es Salaam's natural harbour were not appreciated until the 1870s when the Sultan of Zanzibar built a fort on the banks of the harbour, but the main impetus to growth came from the efforts of the Germans who wished to forestall the British in establishing a 'sphere of influence' around the newly discovered great lakes of the African interior. Control of the coastal area lay in the hands of the Sultan of Zanzibar, but the arrival of five German warships at Zanzibar in August 1885 persuaded him to grant the Germans the use of Dar es Salaam as a base for their colonizing activities in the interior. This date marks the beginning of the city's modern growth. The first imperial governor arrived in 1891, and the next decade saw the building of various administrative offices and the layout of the streets which now characterizes the central area (Figure 8.3). About a kilometre to the west of the 'European' town the colonial authorities laid out, on a rectangular grid-iron street plan, an area for the local porters, who were the mainstay of transport into the interior, to live with their families. Today this is called Kariakoo. Between the two was an area in which Indian traders, mechanics, artisans and clerical workers lived. Thus the morphology of the town was, from the beginning, marked by clear segregation. This pattern has persisted, but currently it has a social rather than a racial basis. The completion in 1914 of the Central Railway from Dar es Salaam to Kigoma on Lake Tanganyika consolidated the city's situation as the centre of the country's administration and economy, and as the chief port. In 1918, following the First World War, Tanganyika came under British rule, and this period has also left its mark on the city.

During the 1920s, the authorities decided to clear the area between Kariakoo and the Indian quarter and to create a broad open space which is now the Freedom Park of Mnazi Mmoja. The displaced population was rehoused in a new suburb at Ilala. To the north of Kariakoo a new suburb was laid out in Upanga for a growing European business community, and north of Msimbazi Bay a large new suburb was created for government servants at Oyster Bay. Port functions were extended south into Mzinga Creek where a special quay was constructed to handle transit trade to the Belgian Congo (now Zaire). Industry was concentrated along the line of the Central Railway to the west of the city. These were the main elements in the morphology of the city at Independence in 1961.

The dominant feature of the post-independence period has been rapid growth achieved by expansion of the city's boundaries and by infilling the areas between the main roads which radiate out from the city centre. Such has been the rapidity of the growth that it has outstripped the abilities of the city authorities to accommodate it in a planned and coordinated manner. Table 8.1 shows some indications of this from the 1978 census. The bulk of the population now lives in unplanned squatter settlements (Figure 8.4). It is estimated that 65% of the 3000 or so new houses which are built annually in the city are on unallocated plots. A total of 60% of the population live in self-built housing units, and squatter settlements are growing at a rate of 13% per annum, compared with 6% in planned areas. The densities are high in squatter areas, often in excess of 300 persons per hectare. These areas have a village-like appearance with single-storey houses constructed of local materials grouped in a haphazard manner, interspersed with small garden plots or 'shambas' where the population grow food crops. Roads are unpaved and there is a lack of basic services. Sewage disposal is on site, and since many squatter settlements are located in areas with poor soil-absorbing properties or a high water table, ponding of effluent may occur and this creates a severe health hazard.

Any city growing as rapidly as Dar es Salaam, currently estimated overall at 8–10% per annum, will experience problems with the supply of essential services as population growth outstrips the ability of the authorities to provide for the people. In a poor country like Tanzania the problems can be severe. Even in areas of the city connected to the mains water system, shortages are frequent, partly because of leakages from the pipes, and partly because people make unofficial

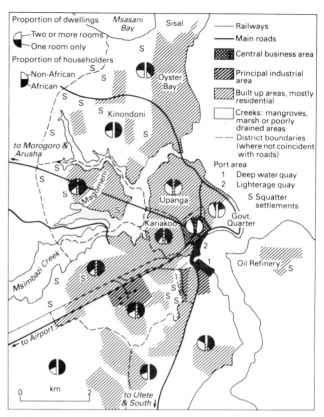

Fig. 8.4 Modern Structure of Dar es Salaam

connections into the system. The excess of demand over supply also applies to the electrical distribution system. The transport system is also under strain because most of the jobs in the formal sector are in the city centre which is the focus for all the main roads. Peak hour traffic congestion is increasingly common. In 1979 less than 20% of the city's total population was employed in the formal sector, leaving the majority in informal activities like petty trading, crafts and domestic service. To provide the basic infrastructure and wage employment for its rapidly growing population, the city is heavily reliant on overseas aid. In the mid-1970s over 60% of all the city's infrastructure projects were foreign-funded. Repayment of foreign debt is a major burden to the country's economy. In 1986 82% of the total annual GNP was owed in debt.

Attempts have been made to slow down the growth of Dar es Salaam, through decentralization to nine regional centres, and by the creation of a new capital at Dodoma. The city continues to grow rapidly, although the rate of increase showed some evidence of slowing down in the late 1988 census, but it could reach three million by the end of the present century, confirming its primacy in the country's urban hierarchy.

ASSIGNMENTS

1. *Why are so many African capital cities located on the coast?*

2. *Describe and attempt to explain the contrasts in degree of urbanization shown in Figure 8.2.*

3. *From Figures 8.3 and 8.4 and the relevant section of text, describe the changing urban structure of Dar es Salaam.*

Table 8.1 Housing stress in Dar es Salaam

	Percentage of Households
With one room dwelling	46%
With water piped to house or plot	31%
With access to own toilet facilities	36%
With 6 or more people	30%

(Source: Census of Tanzania, 1978)

9 Inside a Third World City: Merida, Mexico

M Barke

Introduction

Most urban research within Third World countries has concentrated upon three themes: (i) the extent to which cities are centres of 'modernizing' influences, serving to break down traditional attitudes and practices which may prevent economic and social development; (ii) the impact of social and economic growth on urban form and structure, whereby a 'pre-industrial' arrangement of land uses and social groups is transformed into an internal structure which is similar to that of the cities of the developed West, and, (iii) the problems of providing vital infrastructure for large and rapidly expanding cities.

Despite the concentration on large cities many people in the Third World either live in or depend upon smaller and intermediate urban areas for access to services, goods and markets. Such areas have problems too. This chapter will examine the themes mentioned above for the intermediate sized city of Merida, the capital of the state of Yucatan in south-east Mexico.

Like many urban centres in Latin America, Merida owes its origin to Spanish colonization. It was founded in 1542 by Francisco Montejo and its first citizens were 70 soldiers. The city grew slowly up until the nineteenth century owing to warfare with the indigenous Mayan Indians and disease. By 1803 it was a quiet, provincial city with limited economic functions and a population of about 10 000. Merida's expansion took place after about 1870 with the sudden development of a major industry in Yucatan, the production and manufacture of sisal or henequen fibre. Whilst most of the factories were located outside the city on individual estates, the landowners lived in the city. The peak years were the first decade of the twentieth century when Merida's population increased from 43 630 to 79 426. Subsequently the significance of this industry declined but Merida has continued to grow, reaching 96 660 in 1940, 190 642 in 1960 and 424 529 in 1980. Such rapid growth rates, especially in the 1960s and 1970s, could only be achieved by substantial in-migration. Rapid growth is not just a phenomenon of the very large cities in the Third World.

Population structure

Figure 9.1 shows the age and sex structure of Merida compared with the whole of the state in 1970 and 1980. The classic pyramid, showing a youthful population, is apparent in all cases although the population of Yucatan state is slightly 'younger' in aggregate, 40% aged under 15 in 1980 compared with 35.8% for Merida. This indicates a trend towards a slightly older population in the city, since in 1970 the proportion aged under 15 was 39%. In contrast, the proportion of young adults aged 20–39 increased from 26.1% to 29.4%. Importantly, this is a feature for both males and females. Females in Latin America tend to be equally or more involved in rural-to-urban migration, often for service sector employment – a contrast with the male-dominated rural-to-urban migration in tropical Africa.

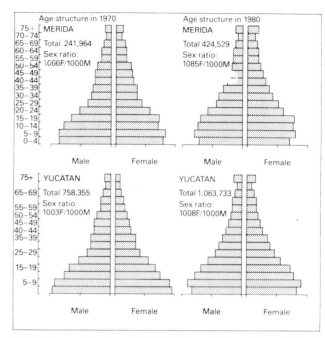

Fig. 9.1 Age and Sex Pyramids, Merida City and Yucatan State, 1970 and 1980

Although high rates of inward migration are a major cause of the recent very rapid growth of Merida, we should not overlook natural increase. The existence of a continued high birth rate is indicated by the ratio of 472 children aged under five years for every 1000 women of child-bearing age (15-44) in 1980. However, the corresponding figure for the rest of the state was 604 per 1000, suggesting that urbanization may be an important influence upon fertility in Third World countries owing to the greater opportunities it offers for female employment and education and the postponement of marriage. Nevertheless, the reproductive capacity of Merida's population remains high (Figure 9.1).

Although the Spanish *conquistadores* were mainly urban dwellers their colonial system required large amounts of native Indian labour. Mayan Indians were therefore settled in Merida and over time some inter-racial mixing took place. By the eighteenth century the upper classes consisted predominantly of a white, exclusively Spanish-speaking elite, although some people of mixed origin had gained acceptance. The lower classes consisted of the Indians and the majority of the mixed population. Economic development in the later nineteenth century brought Merida into much closer contact with the outside world and introduced changes that began to break down the simple class structure based on racial lines. Wealth and achievement became the main criteria for judging social position and a middle class began to emerge, largely independent of racial origin. However, the structure of the population is still strongly influenced by race. One of the main indicators of this is language. Contrary to expectations, Table 9.1 shows that Indian culture is more than surviving in the urban setting. The urban influences of modernization, associated with a nationally-dominant 'Europeanized' elite (Spanish is the official language of education throughout Mexico), do not seem to have eroded older, indigenous traditions. The proportion of the population of Merida who speak an Indian language has increased while there has been a marginal decline throughout Yucatan. The main reason for this unexpected trend is the rapid in-migration of predominantly Mayan-speakers from elsewhere in Yucatan.

Table 9.1 Population aged 5+ speaking an indigenous language (%)

	1970	1980
Speaking Indian Language:		
Yucatan	55.5	54.9
Merida	23.2	25.6
Not speaking Spanish:		
Yucatan	8.8	8.0
Merida	1.0	1.2

(Source: Census of Yucatan, 1970 and 1980)

Table 9.2 Occupational structure in Merida and Yucatan, 1980

	Total Yucatan	Merida
Professional and technical	15 938	12 059
Public officials and officials, managers, administrators and proprietors in private sector	2 701	9 265
Administrative personnel	28 477	22 367
Business people, vendors and related occupations	26 196	16 380
Personal service workers, transportation, etc.	45 462	25 722
Farmers, cattle and timber workers, fishers, etc.	118 133	6 393
Non-agricultural workers, machine operators, etc.	71 073	39 087
Not classified	49 855	18 107
Total economically active	367 825	149 300

(Source: Census of Yucatan, 1980)

Some indication of the present social class structure in Merida can be gained from occupational data (Table 9.2). Approximately half of the economically active population of Merida fall into the lower-class occupations of personal service workers, those employed in agriculture, and lower-grade industrial workers. It is likely that those not specifying an occupation also fall into lower-status categories. Professional and technical workers together with officials and managers in the public and private sectors are counted as middle class and account for a further 14.3%. The administrative personnel category is more problematic since a large proportion is made up of low-grade office workers. Office and sales workers would not be considered genuine middle-class individuals in Merida but they are deemed to occupy a higher position than the lower-class category. These 'lower' middle-class occupations account for a further 26% of Merida's economically active population. As elsewhere in the Third World urbanization is not associated with major industrialization as was the case in nineteenth-century Europe, but the transfer of people out of rural occupations directly into tertiary activities. In Merida only 4.3% of employment is in the primary sector and 26.2% in the secondary (manufacturing and related activities) sector,

leaving over two-thirds of total employment in the service sector. However, Merida contrasts quite substantially with the rest of Yucatan in this respect and it is to the relationship of the city to its region that we must now turn.

Merida and Yucatan state

Population and employment
Merida has always been the only real city in the state of Yucatan. In 1930 it had 22% of the state's inhabitants and in 1980 this had risen to 40%. By the latter date Merida contained 73.4% of Yucatan's managerial and professional workers, 79.5% of the office workers and 54% of those employed in manufacturing industry. Of Yucatan's population receiving more than 22 171 pesos per month (£440 at 1980 prices), 90% live in Merida, and whilst 27% of the economically active in the state receive less than 800 pesos per month (£16 in 1980), in the city this falls to 13.5%. Such contrasts help to explain the very rapid recent inward migration to the city from other parts of the state. Between 1970 and 1980 employment in Yucatan increased by 82.4%, in Merida the corresponding figure was 132%.

Education
Merida also contrasts with much of the rest of Yucatan in social and welfare considerations. Whilst in the state some 15.6% of men (aged over 15) and 22.4% of women are illiterate, the equivalent figures in Merida are 4.8% and 9.2%. Not surprisingly, the proportion of the population with no education whatsoever in Merida is half that of the state. None the less it is interesting that the proportion aged 12 years or over without education is smaller than the proportion aged 6 to 11 years without education both in Merida and across the state. Traditionally, young children have been kept at home and it is after the age of 11 years that some have managed to obtain some education. Clearly, this tendency is still present in the city despite the existence of 'modernizing' influences.

Health
Health criteria also show some startling contrasts. Whilst there are nearly 300 doctors in Merida there are only 40 in the rest of the state. In such circumstances it is surprising that the reported difference in child mortality is not higher. In Merida, women aged over 12 years reported 369 677 live births of which 319 080 were still surviving in 1980, a death rate of 13.7%. In the remainder of Yucatan there were 569 608 reported births of which 479 295 were still surviving, a death rate of 15.8%. However, as these figures depend upon memory

Table 9.3 Income levels in Merida and Yucatan, 1980 (economically active population)

Monthly income	Merida	Yucatan
Less than 800 pesos	20 212	99 768
801 – 3610	41 069	102 464
3611 – 8950	43 928	61 192
8951 – 22170	16 137	20 113
more than 22171	2 831	3 131
not specified	25 203	81 157

(Source: Census of Yucatan, 1980)

they are likely to be rather inaccurate and no account is taken of miscarriages and still-births. None the less, it is surprising that the disparity between the city and the rest of the state is not greater. The death rate is also high in Merida, indicating the existence of significant problems there. Many of these are due to the pressure placed upon housing and basic services in circumstances of rapid growth. Despite this rapid growth there has not automatically been the social change and convergence towards a 'modern' society that might have been expected. To explore the spatial basis of social and economic life in Merida further we must now turn to the changing internal spatial structure of the city.

Layout and land use

Merida was planned on a rectangular grid, according to guidelines which appear to have been universally adopted in the planning of Spanish colonial towns. Despite problems in overcoming Mayan resistance to the *conquistadores* the city had grown to over 200 Spanish households by 1579 with separate *barrios* (districts) on the periphery for the Indian population. This distinction between the centre and the outlying barrios forms the basis of the pre-industrial ecological pattern of most Spanish colonial cities. The focal point was the central square with the four blocks surrounding this occupied by the cathedral, the residence of the leader of the Spanish conquerors, and government buildings. Within two or three blocks of these central functions; the remaining Spaniards were allocated building lots. At this time the centre contained no marketing functions, it was a ceremonial and administrative focus rather than an economic one. Room was left for the expansion of the centre so at some distance beyond the Spanish residential area the *barrios* were established for Indian residence (Figure 9.2a).

A second phase may be identified as beginning from 1870

when the population was about 30 000. The officially recognized 'centre' consisted of 13 blocks from north to south and 10 from east to west (Figure 9.2b). Within this area those highest in social status lived nearest the main square with a downward gradation of social status outwards. Surrounding this 'centre' were five barrios, forming a discontinuous, peripheral ring. Each *barrio* had a depth of from five to eight blocks. Superficially, little change other than physical growth had taken place since the founding of Merida but subtler trends were under way. To the south-east of the central square the principal market was located and around it some permanent shops and businesses had emerged. Most housing was of one storey, masonry-built and often with a central patio. The population was predominantly white but had begun to include some people of mixed race, usually children of a legitimate marriage between Spanish father and Indian mother.

In contrast, the *barrios* were still peopled with Indians. By 1870 five such barrios had emerged, each with its own church and square located on its inner edge, and each tending to copy the social geography of the 'centre'. Those highest in status among the lower classes were located nearest the *barrio* square and social status declined with distance from the centre. Here the similarity ended, for most *barrio* houses were thatched, often one-room dwellings. *Barrio* streets were totally unpaved and unlit.

By about 1940 the distinction between Spaniard and Indian had become less clearly associated with 'upper class' and 'lower class'. Whereas race was previously the sole determinant of social status, by the mid-twentieth century it was only one of several factors, the main one being economic success. This change underlies many of the late nineteenth- and early twentieth-century developments in Merida which were associated with commercial and industrial growth. The latter replaced tradition as the main determinant of urban structure. A more commercially oriented population viewed land and

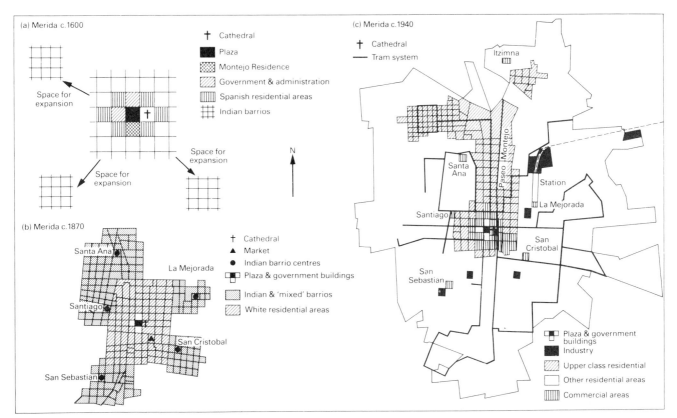

Fig. 9.2 (a) Merida, about 1600 (b) Merida, about 1870 (c) Merida, about 1940

property in a new way – as a financial investment or for the amount of rent it could yield. As the latter depends upon the use to which land and property is put, the value of sites for commercial purposes grew considerably. Technological development, especially in transport, added to the forces for change. Trams (after 1911) and then buses enlarged the potential size of the city and weakened the practical advantages of a residential location at the centre. However, as more economic value was attached to land and property, that value could best be maintained by exclusivity. As the centre, the traditional high-status residential area, was being invaded by commercial land use, that exclusivity was obviously under threat. Thus, in 1901 a new high-status residential sector was developed along the wide, tree-lined Paseo Montejo (Figure 9.2c), the main road leading north from the centre of Merida through the Santa Ana barrio to the port of Progreso. Huge, luxurious mansions were built and this development began to break down the old centre–barrio distinction.

The centre came to be increasingly a business district, based upon the central square and extending about six blocks from east to west and five from north to south. Initially, shops and offices were located in converted upper-class houses but gradually purpose-built structures began to emerge. By 1940 secondary business centres had also begun to develop elsewhere in the city, especially around the former barrio squares (Figure 9.2C). The most important of these centres contained about 30 business establishments. In the Santa Ana *barrio* to the north, adjacent to the new high status sector. To the west, development around the square of the Santiago *barrio* was of similar size. In the poorer south-west district of San Sebastian only about six commercial establishments were found around the square and similarly modest levels occurred at San Cristobal in the south-east and Mejorada to the north-east. In addition some small business centres had begun to emerge in former villages which, as a result of developments in transport, were becoming residential suburbs.

The nature and construction of houses had also begun to change. Although small, rural-type thatched dwellings still remained at the edge of the city, masonry houses increased rapidly (even in the poorer districts) nearer the centre. Much

of the city was taking on a more 'urban' appearance. Despite this, no major industrial sector had emerged: although the location of the railway station and goods yards in the north-eastern sector had tended to pull most of the larger factories in that general direction, smaller units were scattered over much of the rest of the urban area.

By the 1980s many of these trends of change from a pre-industrial, 'traditional' city to a more modern, commercially-oriented urban area had been reinforced. Merida still contains many elements from the past and it is far from being a modern industrial city, but in the principal elements and processes that determine its spatial structure it is well on the way in a transition to the latter. Enormous population growth has enlarged the city but placed considerable pressure on available services, especially housing. A fully-fledged central business district (CBD) has emerged and expanded although high-rise development is still not prevalent. Further commercial expansion has taken place along two 'ribbons', one along the Paseo Montejo containing banks, hotels, restaurants and other entertainments, and one in the south-west on the road to Campeche, located near the airport and a further new development – an industrial estate. Industrial land use has grown generally throughout the city, but peripheral locations suitable for motorized transport are most common, especially in this south-western sector.

By the 1980s the centre had become almost exclusively a commercial area with few residential properties. The upper-class residential area has continued to grow northwards (Figure 9.3) to include one or two exclusive residential developments which were built in the 1970s. Peripheral areas of the city, apart from those in the north, are characterized by low-status residential areas, a common feature of most Third World cities. Many of these developments are, of course, illegal and the result of squatting, where the residents lay out and build their own dwellings. This growth has accelerated with the rapid recent growth of population in Merida and the inability of the city authorities to cope with the influx. It is to this aspect that we must finally turn.

Housing problems

In 1979 official estimates calculated that Merida had a housing deficit of 9217 units of accommodation to house families who, literally, were 'without houses'. A further 4645 units were required to replace houses in a dangerous or deteriorated condition, and 2237 units were needed for the relief of overcrowding in existing dwellings. The 1980 census gives a population of 424 529 living in 84 097 houses, or 5.05 people per house. It must also be noted that 70% of all dwellings are of three rooms or less (14.5% of one room only) and 72% have only one or two bedrooms. Therefore overcrowding is a severe problem. The wider significance of crowding is perhaps best appreciated in relation to issues such as access to drinking water and sewage disposal. Although 93% of houses in Merida have access to electric power, some 36% have no direct water supply and only 5% have connection into the public sewage disposal system. A further 49% rely on septic tanks and 35% have no effective sewage disposal whatsoever. Furthermore, a survey in 1979 found that about 60% of the water supply available through public pumps and wells was lost through leaks and that the health of one quarter of the city's population was directly affected by inadequate water supply and sewage disposal.

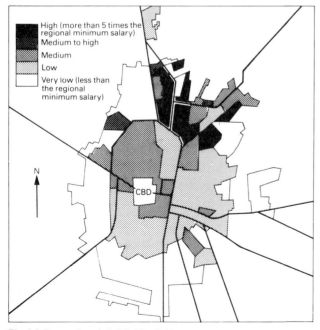

High (more than 5 times the regional minimum salary)
Medium to high
Medium
Low
Very low (less than the regional minimum salary)

Fig. 9.3 Income Levels in Merida, 1980

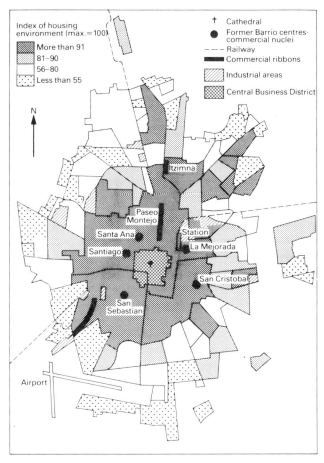

Fig. 9.4 Housing Quality in Merida, 1980

Table 9.4 Relationship between income levels and index of housing environmental quality

Index of housing environmental quality (100 = maximum)	Income levels		
	Very low	Low	Medium/high
80 – 100	4	11	16
60 – 80	13	3	7
60	19	1	1

Table 9.5 Relationship between housing age and index of housing environmental quality

When built	Percentage of housing areas scoring			
	80 – 100	60 – 80	40 – 60	40
Before 1900	100.0	–	–	–
1900-1950	46.1	34.6	15.5	3.8
1950-1960	16.7	66.6	–	16.7
1960-1970	21.4	21.4	21.4	35.8
After 1970	11.1	11.1	33.3	44.5

(Source: Instituto de Virienda: Merida; Diagnostico de Vivienda)

Figure 9.4 shows an index of the environmental quality of housing areas based on the presence or absence of such things as water, drainage, lighting, electric power, etc. It is clear that those areas scoring lowest on this index tend to be peripheral in their location, but they are discontinuous. Also, some low-scoring areas are located adjacent to areas of considerably higher quality. Furthermore, comparing Figure 9.3 with Figure 9.4 shows that there is no direct correspondence between broad income areas and housing quality. To a large extent this is because many of the areas of low-quality, illegal squatter housing are quite small and located near to housing of reasonable quality with reasonable facilities. In many cases this is a deliberate and clever policy on the part of illegal squatters for it is easier for them eventually to connect into the power, water and drainage services, either officially or unofficially.

A final question which must be answered concerns the possibility of improvement for such areas. A number of studies of poor housing areas in Latin America have suggested that, over time, a gradual improvement is likely to take place, provided the circumstances are right. Included in the latter are access to some form of employment and therefore income, and security of tenure and/or land holding. Although the initial housing development may have been illegal the granting of some form of security may encourage residents gradually to up-grade the area for themselves. Table 9.4 shows that there is a very broad relationship for all areas between income levels and quality of housing environment and Table 9.5 indicates that the younger the housing areas, the lower the environmental quality is likely to be, but that improvement may well take place over time. However, security of tenure is important for if we take the 37 housing areas in the 'very low income' category, 19 are legal and 18 illegal. Of the latter, 15 score less

than 60 on the housing environment index but of the former only five. Thus, legality and the security it brings would appear to be an important factor in housing improvement even in very low income areas. It may well be, therefore, that the problems of meeting housing demand can be met by recognizing the existence of squatter settlements and providing basic services, rather than ignoring them altogether.

Conclusion

If we return to the three themes that have dominated the study of very large cities in the Third World, it is clear that in some respects an intermediate-sized city like Merida differs from larger places but in others it is similar. Whilst 'modernizing' influences are undoubtedly present in Merida there are a number of 'traditional' aspects which appear to be surviving quite successfully, most notably the Mayan language. The land use structure and social geography of the city demonstrate definite change from a pre-industrial pattern yet the transition is, as yet, far from complete. Finally, even though Merida is not a huge agglomeration like Mexico City it too exhibits considerable symptoms of urban stress, related especially to the provision of housing and other basic infrastructure.

ASSIGNMENTS
---

1. *With reference to Table 9.2 calculate the differences in occupational structure between Merida and the rest of the state of Yucatan. Comment on the significance of these differences.*

2. *Using the text and Figures 9.2, 9.3 and 9.4 comment on how the spatial structure of Merida differs from the classical models of urban spatial structure known to you.*

3. *To what extent do Tables 9.4 and 9.5 indicate that low income housing areas in Merida are likely to improve over time? Comment on the factors which may assist such improvement.*

10 Nepal: Demographic Trends and Patterns

M Sill

Introduction

Nepal is a small Himalayan country located between two giant neighbours, China to the north and India to the south. About 800 kilometres long and 200 kilometres wide, the country can be divided into three broad physical zones of varying population densities, the Mountain zone, the Hill zone and the Terai, (Figure 10.1). In the high, inhospitable Himalayan Mountain zone, above 3000 metres high, population densities are low, averaging about 25 per square kilometre, and fall to under 5 per square kilometre in the highest districts. In the intermediate Hill zone, between 900 and 3000 metres, population densities are much higher, averaging 120 per square kilometre. There is acute population pressure on the available agricultural land: in some Hill districts, for example, there are as many as 1500 people per square kilometre of cultivated land. To the south of the Hills lies the Nepalese Terai. This lowland area is the flat northern part of the great Gangetic plain. Up to the 1950s most of the Terai was sparsely populated malarious forest, but since then, with the virtual eradication of malaria, the Terai has been rapidly settled both by Mountain and Hill Nepalis, and by Indians from adjoining states. As a result of rapid population growth, most of the Terai is now under cultivation for rice, wheat and cash crops such as sugar and oil seeds; much of the forest has disappeared, and the population density averages 200 per square kilometre. Table 10.1 summarizes some of the population and demographic characteristics of the country.

Nepal is one of the poorest countries in the world, with an average income per head of only $180 in 1988. Almost all Nepalis still work on the land, with 93 per cent listed as farmers in the 1981 census. Only 6.4 per cent of the population was urban in 1981, although the urban component is growing rapidly at an annual rate of 7.6 per cent. Nepal shares many of

Table 10.1 NEPAL: Selected demographic patterns by physical zone

	Mountain	Hill	Terai	Total
Population in millions (1981)	1.3	7.1	6.6	15
Per cent of total	8.7	47.7	43.6	100
Density per sq km	25	117	193	102
Average annual population increase rates				
1961-71	(1.85)		2.39	2.05
1971-81	1.35	1.63	4.11	2.62
Fertility rates				
1971	541	575	616	587
1981	617	643	680	656

(Source: Population monograph of Nepal, 1987)

the demographic characteristics of other low-income countries, such as a high birth rate, falling crude death and infant mortality rates, an increase in life expectation, an accelerating rate of population growth, and a youthful population.

General demographic features

In overall terms, the crude birth rate in Nepal was about 42:1000 in the early 1980s: it has remained largely unchanged over the last twenty years, and there is little evidence of any recent reduction. Expressing fertility another way, women in Nepal can expect to have six surviving children by the end of their reproductive life span, i.e. the total fertility rate = 6. In a traditional peasant society such as Nepal, children are still seen as an economic asset, providing extra pairs of hands for work about the farm. Furthermore, the adoption of artificial means of contraception is not yet widespread; only 15% of married women were recorded as users in 1986, so families tend to be large. The virtual eradication of some killer diseases such as malaria and smallpox, and the spread of health posts offering primary health care, have contributed to a fall in crude death rates in Nepal from 24:1000 in 1965 to 15:1000 in 1988. Infant mortality rates, too, have fallen from 182:1000 live births in 1964 to estimates which vary between 110-126:1000 in 1988. Maternal mortality rates, at 850:100 000 live births in 1986, remain very high by Third World standards, partly because of the low incidence, only 10%, of births attended by health staff, together with low standards of hygiene and nutrition in many parts of Nepal. However, with the reduction of the crude death rate, there has been an increase in life expectation at birth, from 37 years in 1961 to 51 years in 1988. Male life expectancy, at 52 years, is higher than female, at 50 years. This finding is similar to those for Pakistan and Bangladesh, and reflects the higher social and economic status of men in traditional Nepalese society. Related to the higher male life expectancy, the sex-ratio is also male-dominant, with 105 males per 100 females recorded in the 1981 census. This pattern occurs despite the continuation of male-specific

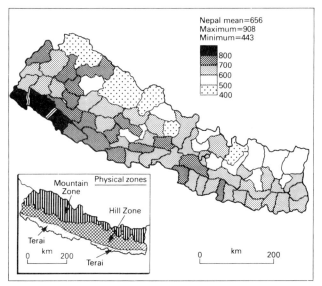

Fig. 10.1 Physical Zones of Nepal (inset) and Distribution of Fertility Rates, 1981

Nepal mean=656
Maximum=908
Minimum=443

800
700
600
500
400

Physical zones
Mountain Zone
Hill Zone
Terai
km 200
km 200
Terai

net emigration from Nepal, without which the sex-ratio would be even more weighted to the males. As a consequence of a sustained high birth rate and falling mortality levels, Nepal is experiencing an acceleration of the rate of population increase, from an annual average of 2.0% between 1961 and 1971, to 2.6% per year during the decade 1971-1981. At the same time, Nepalese society remains youthful with 41% aged between 0-14, 49.8% under 20 years, 66% under 30 years and only 3.25% aged 65 and over.

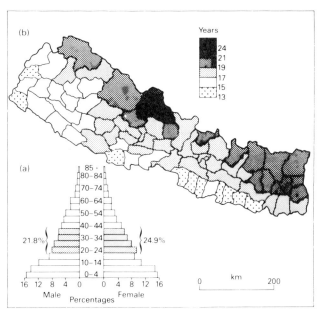

Fig. 10.2 (a) Age and Sex Pyramid for Nepal, 1981 and (b) Mean Age at Marriage of Females, 1981

Several of Nepal's demographic characteristics are summarized in the population pyramid, Figure 10.2(a). Its overall shape is determined by fertility rates, by mortality rates and by patterns of international migration. High fertility rates explain the broad base of the pyramid. High mortality rates until recent years have caused a steep reduction of the numbers in each successive age cohort, leaving the elderly as a small part of the total population. The diagram also shows that, unlike that for the total population, the sex-ratio is female dominant between the ages of 20 and 39. The proportion of all men in this age range is 21.8%, somewhat below the female figure of 24.5%. This probably reflects the effect of international emigration, which is age and sex specific. Economically active Nepalese males in particular seek employment abroad in India, the Gulf States or as Gurkha soldiers in the British and Indian armies. Somewhat unexpectedly, more women are recorded in the 20–24 age group than in the 15–19 cohort. This probably results from young mothers reporting a higher age to the census official in order to enhance their esteem. Similarly, an under-recording of 55–59-year-old women is probably due to elderly females exaggerating their age in an attempt to raise their social status. Finally, high fertility rates and increased life expectation levels produce high and increasing dependency ratios, as greater numbers of children and elderly have to be supported by those of working age. In Nepal today, 100 workers support 90 dependants, whereas thirty years ago they supported 77, and this upward trend is likely to continue. In contrast, the dependency ratio in most developed countries is in the 45–60 years range.

Regional and local scales: fertility

At the regional and local scale it is possible to identify spatial and temporal variations in fertility levels as measured by the fertility rate, expressed as:

$$\frac{\text{Children 0–4 years}}{\text{Women 15–49 years}} \times 1000.$$

The recorded increase in the national fertility rate shown in Table 10.1 could reflect a more thorough enumeration of children in the 1981 census, as well as a fall in the infant mortality rate, rather than an actual increase in overall fertility levels. The lower fertility rates in the Mountain zone, compared with the Terai in particular, are probably explained by factors such as higher infant mortality rates in the harsh mountain environment, by the net out-migration of young adults, particularly males, and by the incidence of higher female marriage ages (see below). At the district scale, the pattern of fertility rates is complex. Figure 10.1 shows that most of the Mountain districts record fertility levels well below the national average. This is also found in the eastern Hill districts, from which many males have migrated to the Terai. Above average fertility rates are found in the Terai districts, particularly in the recently settled western section. This area continues to experience large-scale immigration from the western Mountains and Hills, a growing stream of migrants from the longer-settled eastern Terai, as well as impoverished Indian peasants seeking land cleared from the remaining forest.

A statistical analysis of the district level variation in the fertility rate indicated that the two most important explanatory variables were female marriage patterns and the urban proportion in the population of the district. In the case of the former, female marriage patterns have an important bearing on fertility rates, especially in a traditional peasant society like Nepal, where artificial contraception is not widespread, and in which most births take place within marriage. In such societies, delayed marriage is the principal fertility control, and this can be measured by the marriage rate (i.e. the proportion of females in Nepal over ten years old who are married, divorced or widowed) and by the age at marriage.

In terms of the marriage rate, Table 10.2 shows significant regional variations which can be compared with variations in fertility levels. In the Mountain and Hill zones, the lower marriage rates are probably explained by male-dominant out-migration and correspond with higher marriage ages than in the Terai, where the marriage rate is very high. The lowest marriage rate is in the highly urbanized Kathmandu Valley, which could well reflect the migration of young single people to the major towns in the Valley, Kathmandu, Patan and

Table 10.2 NEPAL: Selected female demographic characteristics

1981	Nepal	Mountain	Hill	Kathmandu Valley	Terai
Ever-married females as percentage of females 10 years+	76.7	73.4	74.4	71.5	80.2
Mean age at marriage for females 10 years+	17.2	18.5	18.0	18.8	15.8

*Ever-married = married, divorced or widowed

(Source: Population monograph of Nepal, 1987)

Bhaktapur, where traditional peasant attitudes to early marriage are breaking down.

With reference to the age of marriage of females, the mean age in 1981 was 17.2 years: amongst urban women the age was 18.5 years, compared with 17.1 years for rural females. This deferral of marriage on the part of urban women can be linked to lower fertility levels in Nepalese towns. At the regional scale, the lowest mean ages of marriage for women are found in the Terai, particularly in the eastern section where mean ages of under 15 or even under 14 are found in some districts (Figure 10.2(b) and Table 10.2). Marriages are deferred longest in the Mountain districts (Manang district = 24.8 years), and in the eastern Hill districts, due, at least in part, to the heavy exodus of youthful, male-dominant migrants from these areas.

Cultural variables

Recent demographic research in Nepal has identified a series of cultural and economic variables which help to explain these spatial variations in marriage patterns. First, the more highly educated women, employed in administrative, clerical or professional capacities, and mostly living in towns, are more likely to defer marriage than women with little or no schooling. The mean marriage age for women who completed secondary education is 20 years, compared with 17 years for the majority of females with no education at all. Secondly, female marriage ages vary with religious adherence. The mean marriage age of female Buddhists is 18.9 years, for Hindus (the majority of the population), 17.2 years, whilst for female Muslims it is as early as 14.8 years. As Nepal's Buddhist population is found chiefly in the central and eastern Hills, this may help to explain the relatively high female marriage ages in these districts. In contrast, the concentration of early-marrying Muslims in the Terai probably contributes towards the low female marriage ages found in this zone. Thirdly, there is an inverse association between the sex-ratio and the mean age of female marriage. The higher the proportion of males in a given district, the lower the female age at marriage tends to be: hence the prevalence of early marriages in the male-dominant Terai and the reverse in the Mountain and Hill zones, from which long-distance, male-dominant migration streams have flowed. In the case of the towns, urban fertility was only 67% of rural fertility in the late 1970s, because of factors such as lower urban marriage rates and the greater availability of contraceptive aids.

Mortality differentials

Owing to the limitations of the data, analysis of mortality trends is possible only at the crudest of spatial scales. Nepal, like many other Third World countries, does not have a long-established system of collecting demographic statistics. The vital registration system was established as recently as 1977. Non-reportage in remote rural and mountainous areas means that the quality of data on infant mortality rates, on causes of death and even on age at death, is likely to be defective. It would appear, however, that crude death rates were much higher in rural areas than in towns, 18:1000 per year compared with 12:1000 in the early 1980s. Unlike Western cities during the industrial revolution, where mortality rates were much higher than in the countryside, urban centres in Nepal experience much lower death rates than do rural areas. This is largely because public and private health services and facilities are concentrated in the towns: half of Nepal's 750 doctors live

Table 10.3 Infant mortality rates, 1962 – 1981

	Urban	Rural	Mountain	Hill	Terai
1962	127	185	190	170	184
1981	67	135	186	142	122

(Source: Population monograph of Nepal, 1987)

in, or around, the capital Kathmandu. Furthermore, a higher proportion of the urban population has above-average education and income levels, so facilitating their access to medical services as well as ensuring better housing and nutritional levels than most rural dwellers. For much the same reasons, infant mortality rates too are lower in the towns, as Table 10.3 shows. Whilst infant mortality rates have fallen in the countryside, due in part to the spread of rural health posts, urban infant mortality rates have fallen more rapidly since the early 1960s. Persistently high infant mortality rates in the Mountain zone reflect remoteness from health care, extreme poverty and harsh climatic conditions. The significant decline in the infant mortality rate in the Terai is probably due to easier access to medical services, somewhat higher income levels and a growing urban component in the total population. As an illustration of the problems inherent in any analysis of demographic trends in Nepal, current estimates of the infant mortality rate vary from 128:1000 per year (World Bank Development Report, 1987) to 110:1000 (Nepal Demographic Sample Survey, 1986/87). The World Bank estimate could be the more accurate of the two because of the restricted size of the mid-decennial sample survey, but whatever the figure, the fact remains that the infant mortality rate in Nepal is still high by international standards – almost twice the average for all low-income countries of 76:1000 in 1987.

Given the inferior social and economic status of women in Nepalese society, in which they are expected to perform arduous physical work on the land or portering, as well as child-bearing and domestic tasks, it is to be expected that female mortality rates are higher than male. Nepal is one of the few countries in the world where female life expectation is lower than male, and as a result, the sex-ratio is male dominant. In 1981, the ratio was 105, which means that for every 100 Nepalese women there were 105 men. In every age group except 20–34, males outnumber females. For the 65–69 age group the sex-ratio is as high as 116, reflecting the greater life expectancy of Nepalese men. Only in the prime working ages of 20–34 do females outnumber males because of male dominant emigration of young adult men. At the regional scale, there is an excess of males in each of the three ecological zones, but the sex-ratio, at 108, is highest in the Terai, compared with 104 in the Mountain zone and 102 in the Hill zone. The most likely explanation is inter-regional migration. For example, the sex-ratio of life-time immigrants to the Terai in 1981 was 111.5, whilst the sex-ratio of out-migrants from the Mountains and Hills was 107.1 and 108.2 respectively. Clearly, males were more prone to migrate longer distances from zone to zone in search of land, urban employment or education: females were more likely to migrate shorter distances, within the ecological zones, with marriage as the major motive. In terms of urban-rural sex-ratios, the population of Nepal's towns is strongly masculine, with a ratio of 115 in 1981. This again is largely explained by male migration to towns from the countryside. This is supported by the lower sex-ratios, between 90 and 95, observed for working age groups in the rural areas, particularly amongst the 20–34 age group. However, it needs to be remembered that the reduced proportion of young adult males in the Nepalese countryside is also due, at least in part, to international emigration.

Age structures

The age structure of a population is important, not just for demographic purposes, but as a basis for population forecasting, to assist the planning of investment in sectors such as employment, health and education. Unfortunately for Nepal, the quality of the census data on ages is not very reliable. Ages, in many cases, are not accurately known, as the compulsory registration of births has been introduced only recently. Instead, estimates of individuals' ages are often obtained from significant life events, such as marriage, or from people's physical characteristics. Bearing these limitations in mind, the age structure of the population of Nepal is shown in Figure 10.2(a). Differences in the age structure of rural and urban areas can also be identified, with the towns somewhat over-represented in the 15–24 age group and the rural areas in the 0–14 and 60+ age groups. In the case of the latter, the higher proportion of children in rural areas may reflect higher fertility levels, while the higher incidence of elderly people could be due to the existence of strong family ties in the ancestral home. In the towns, the higher proportion of young adults may be attributed to the movement of such people from rural areas in search of work, education or training. At the regional scale, the Terai is over-represented in the 0–14 age range and under-represented at the 60+ stage. These patterns could be due, respectively, to higher fertility rates in the Terai and to the recency of much of the migration to the Terai by youthful Nepalis and Indians.

Conclusion

In conclusion, it can be seen that major changes are occurring in Nepal's population dynamics. Traditionally, the majority of the population lived in the Mountains and Hills: tough and resourceful villagers who cultivated terraced hillslopes, and who grazed sheep and goats in the upland valleys. In the first census, conducted between 1952 and 1954, 65% of the population lived in the Mountains and Hills, whilst 35% of the population lived in the Terai; only 2.8% of the population was urban. By 1981, the proportion living in the Mountains and Hills had fallen to 53%, with 47% recorded in the narrow southern lowland strip, the Terai; the urban component had increased to 6.4%. If the population changes identified in the 1981 census are projected to the end of the century, it can be argued that Nepal will be transformed, within a generation, from being an archetypal Hill and Mountain society to a plains–urban nation. By projecting the 1971–1981 population growth rate of the Terai, 4.11% per year, to 2001, 56% of the population will be living in the flat, sub-tropical plain. The figure rises to 60% if the projected urban population of the Hills is added to the total Terai population. At the national scale, a projection of the 1970s urban growth rate, 7.6% per year, suggests that 20% of the population will be town dwellers by the beginning of the next century, some five million people, compared with 958 000 in 1981. Even after allowing for a slow-down in these projected growth rates, the population trends are clear. An increasing proportion of a rapidly growing population will be seeking work, housing and other services in the Terai and in towns and cities. As the focus for development policies has, for several decades, been rural development in the Hills and Mountains, it remains to be seen whether the government can redirect its economic and social development plans to address the problems inherent in current and projected demographic changes.

ASSIGNMENTS

1. *At which stage of the demographic transition model is Nepal today? Justify your choice of stage.*

2. *With reference to Nepal, illustrate the statement that the demographic structure of a population depends upon both natural and migrational components of change.*

---

11 Migration in Tanzania: Testing some Basic Models

M Barke and J C Sowden

Introduction: models of migration

Migration is a topic of immense importance in most Third World countries and is usually described in terms of rural-to-urban movement. However, as Figure 11.1 indicates, this is not the only form of migration.

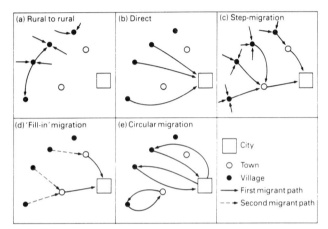

Fig. 11.1 Types of Migration in the Third World

Although frequently discounted, we should not forget that a large proportion of migration in Third World countries takes place *within* rural areas. Secondly, there is direct migration from rural areas to large cities. In many Third World countries, just one city is so large and dominant (primate) that it is the destination for the vast majority of rural-to-urban migrants. In other words there is just one migration 'field' comprising the whole of the national territory. In other cases, however, the movement is much more gradual, and takes place in a series of stages or steps. It may begin when the rural dweller moves from village to the nearest town, continuing with a move to the provincial capital, then on to the main city. In such cases the urban hierarchy is paralleled by a hierarchy of migration fields, ranging from the localized sphere of a small town 'nesting' within the larger sphere of a provincial capital to that capital's subservience in turn to the major city's migration field. A variant of step-migration is 'fill-in' migration, where as people move from smaller urban centres to larger, an opportunity is left for a 'new' rural-to-urban migrant to fill. Finally, circular migration occurs where the stay in the urban area is only temporary and the migrant returns to his/her rural home. We should not expect one model or one type of migration to be equally applicable to all individuals and groups in the same country for examples of several kinds of migration may be found in the same country. In Africa especially, we may expect quite marked differences between male and female migration for a variety of reasons. There is greater opportunity for waged employment for males in urban areas, traditionally much of women's work has been concerned with agriculture and maintaining the family land and, in colonial times, female migration to urban areas was actively discouraged. In contrast we may expect more females to be rural-to-rural migrants, if only for marriage reasons.

Tanzania provides a useful case to test these models of migration since it possesses a primate city in Dar es Salaam (Table 11.1), more than five times the size of the next largest city (Mwanza) in 1978 and with a population of 1 360 850 in 1988. Thus the basic immaturity of the urban hierarchy may lead us to expect that step-migration is limited and *direct* migration to the primate city more pronounced. On the other hand, provincial centres do exist and, as Tanzania is a very large country, may well represent intervening opportunities for migrants. We shall attempt to examine migration in Tanzania in relation to the theoretical models using data principally from the censuses of 1967 and 1978. Initially, however, it is necessary to provide some background context.

Table 11.1 Growth of urban centres in Tanzania, 1957–1988

	1957	1967	1978	1988*
Arusha	10 038	32 452	86 845	117 622
Bukoba	5 297	8 141	77 022	28 702
Dar es Salaam	128 742	272 821	851 522	1 234 754
Dodoma	13 435	23 559	159 577	88 473
Iringa	9 587	21 746	57 182	84 860
Kigoma-Ujiji	16 255	21 369	58 788	77 055
Lindi	10 315	13 352	27 308	41 587
Mbeya	6 932	12 479	78 111	135 614
Morogoro	14 507	25 262	74 114	117 760
Moshi	13 726	26 864	52 223	96 838
Musoma	4 937	15 412	43 980	63 652
Mtwara-Mikindani	10 459	20 413	48 510	76 632
Mwanza	19 877	34 861	169 660	182 899
Shinyanga	–	–	68 746	63 471
Singida	–	–	55 892	39 598
Songea	–	–	49 303	54 830
Sumbawanga	–	–	57 802	47 878
Tabora	15 361	21 012	67 392	93 506
Tanga	38 053	61 058	143 878	138 274

	1978	1988
N.B. Zanzibar	110 611	157 634

* Excluding 'rural' wards.

(Sources: Censuses of Tanzania, 1967 and 1978)

Background to migration in Tanzania

Migration is not a new phenomenon in Tanzania, although its scale and causes have changed greatly over the past hundred years. In the early nineteenth century, nomadic groups such as the Masai were in the final stages of a long-term migration from the Ethiopian Highlands into East Africa where they came into contact and conflict with the already established Bantu peoples. The south of Tanzania was affected by the aggressive incursions of the Angoni from southern Africa during this same period. But both of these occurred as part of large-scale and long-term movements which were not economically motivated in the modern sense. Tanzania was generally lightly settled at this time and its economy was subsistence-based.

However, by about 1850 parts of the country were becoming involved with external forces which laid the basis of the contemporary, wage-based economy. The East African coast has a long history of Arab urban settlement (Chapter 8) and Bagamoyo and Zanzibar were bases from which expeditions and slave caravans led into the interior. But it was only after 1885, under German colonial influence, that railways, commercial farms, plantations and towns developed. However, the population of Dar es Salaam was only 5000 in 1886, growing to 18 000 by 1900. In the twentieth century there came a demand for wage labour, and the beginnings of migration from the more remote and environmentally harsher parts of the country to the newly growing towns and to the areas of commercial agriculture (especially sisal estates) which were developing in locations accessible to the railways.

By the time of Independence in 1961 an uneven spatial pattern of development had emerged. This pattern, with large 'empty' areas in the west and south of the country and 'islands' of development around the periphery, reflects environmental and historical factors. The main areas of commercial development are the better watered highlands of the North and South, and the Lake Victoria shorelands, which produce cash crops such as sisal, coffee, tea and cotton. The less developed regions have large tracts of dense tse-tse infested bush which make settlement by people and the raising of cattle impossible. The main migration streams can be understood with reference to this pattern of economic activity, with movement into those rural areas where commercial farming had developed, and into the towns, especially Dar es Salaam.

After Independence, the pace of rural-to-urban migration began to increase, but since the bulk of the population – over 80% – was engaged in agriculture, the government concentrated on this sector in its early development plans. Three types of economic region had evolved: (i) areas specializing in the production of cash crops for export; (ii) areas adjacent to and supplying the cash crop and urban centres with food crops and services; (iii) peripheral areas which were stagnating and acting as reservoirs of migrant labour to (i) and (ii). Rural incomes were low and many people were remote from basic necessities such as piped water, schools and health centres. Because the bulk of the population lived in small, dispersed settlements (widely scattered throughout the country), any schemes to provide them with their basic needs would be costly. As a result the government adopted a policy of villagization to try to address this situation. This involved the grouping of the rural population into villages of about 250 families.

At first the government adopted a policy of voluntary villagization. The new villages began to appear during 1967–8. After 1973, however, villagization became compulsory for the entire rural population. In 1974 three million people were compulsorily moved into villages, in many cases only weeks before planting was due. This bureaucratic mis-management, added to the problems of drought which were affecting the country at this time, contributed to a severe shortfall in domestic food production. Thus the policy of villagization brought about a kind of enforced rural-to-rural migration for many people. Estimates in the later 1970s suggest that about eight or nine million people (Tanzania's population in 1978 was 17.1 million) were moved. However, the vast majority of these moves were short-distance; the average in Iringa district, for example, was only 4.9 km.

Despite this and other policies which attempted to check the outward flow of migrants from poorer rural areas, it appears that such movements have persisted. The remainder of this chapter will examine the form that such movement takes, with particular emphasis on the nature of rural-to-urban moves and the applicability of models B or C in Figure 11.1.

Migration from the 1967 census

Table 11.2 shows the main categories of movement for each region. Short-range migration (intra-regional) predominates. The likelihood is that much of this is rural-to-rural migration or movement to local urban or regional centres. It is possible that the latter could represent the first stage of step-migration. Figure 11.2 shows for the 16 largest towns in Tanzania the first, second, and third largest flows from their regions of origin. In 14 cases the largest inflow is from within the regions in which these towns are situated (for this purpose, Dar es Salaam was counted as being in Coast region). It appears that,

Table 11.2 Mainland Tanzania: Mobility of regional populations, 1967. (percentage born outside locality of residence)

Region	Intra-regional migration	Inter-regional migration	Overall mobility
Tabora	45.0	16.9	61.9
Shinyanga	47.9	12.3	60.2
Singida	40.4	14.8	55.2
Ruvuma	38.1	12.7	50.8
Mara	37.3	6.5	43.8
West Lake	36.1	6.1	42.2
Kigoma	31.5	11.0	42.5
Mtwara	36.0	5.8	41.8
Arusha	36.4	4.7	41.1
Morogoro	30.6	9.8	40.4
Coast (inc.Dar)	30.5	6.6	37.5
Tanga	29.6	7.7	37.3
Mbeya	30.2	6.7	36.9
Dodoma	26.9	7.1	34.0
Iringa	17.9	8.3	26.2
Mwanza	12.1	14.1	26.2
Kilimanjaro	14.3	8.1	22.4
All regions	30.8	9.2	40.0

(Source: Census of Tanzania, 1967)

Fig. 11.2 Tanzania's Largest Urban Areas, 1967: Regions of Origin of Migrants

for most of the towns of Tanzania, the largest numbers of in-migrants are relatively short-distance. However, to prove that step-migration does take place it is necessary to demonstrate that the major outflows from these urban areas are to larger towns and especially to Dar es Salaam. Unfortunately, the available data from both the 1967 and 1978 censuses do not enable us to test this as they contain data on the *regions* of origin of migrants only, not urban areas of origin. Any analysis of step-migration in Tanzania has therefore to be based on indirect indicators. However, Table 11.2 and Figure 11.2 allow us to reach the preliminary conclusion for 1967 that much migration was short-range, composed of rural-to-rural moves and flows from rural areas to regional capitals. The latter is consistent with the first stages of step-migration. It is possible that a larger number of migrants are involved in direct migration to Dar es Salaam, since Figure 11.2 simply shows the sources of the largest flows *into* each of the towns.

Table 11.3 shows the proportion of the population of the main towns in 1967 who were born elsewhere. It is clear that a very large proportion of urban dwellers were migrants although these people could have moved into the towns shown at any stage of their lives. Importantly, the primate city of Dar es Salaam differs little from the other towns in its proportion of migrants. Were it the case that the majority of migration in Tanzania was directly from rural area to primate city (type B), then the other towns in Table 11.3 would show much lower proportions of migrants. This is clearly not the case. All the towns listed appear to receive quite substantial in-flows of population.

Figure 11.3 shows the destinations of the largest migrant flows from each region together with the number of migrants to Dar es Salaam from each region. Dar es Salaam is different from other towns both numerically and in terms of the extent of its migration field, for it receives over 1000 migrants from each of the 18 regions. Remarkably, this includes some of the more distant regions such as West Lake, Tabora, Mbeya and Ruvuma. These are amongst the most poorly developed areas in Tanzania and we may hypothesize that direct migration to the primate city is more likely from the poorer regions. In the more developed areas of the north-east and north-west, short-

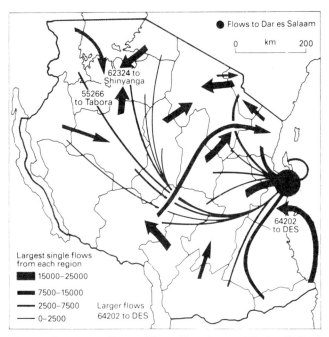

Fig. 11.3 Destination of Largest Migrant Flows from each Region, 1967 and Number of Migrants to Dar es Salaam from each Region

range migration to regional centres could be more attractive. It is still possible, however, that such a move could be part of step-migration towards Dar es Salaam.

Finally, the sex-ratio of rural-to-urban migrants is of interest. Nationally, there were 1050 women for every 1000 men in 1967. For all migrants (those born outside the locality they were enumerated in) there were 1083 women for every 1000 men, but for the four towns of Iringa, Mbeya, Mwanza and Dar es Salaam the ratios were 856, 956, 736 and 752 respectively. Therefore, although women were overall considerably more migratory than men, they were much less likely to move to urban areas. Most female migration was within the same region, predominantly of type A, and it is males who predominate in the longer-distance inter-regional and rural-to-urban movements.

Migration as shown by the 1978 census

Unfortunately the 1978 census of Tanzania is not comparable with that of 1967 and therefore it is not possible to parallel the above analysis. The major shortcoming of the 1978 census is that migration is not directly measured for *urban* places (with the exception of Dar es Salaam). Most data is on a regional basis only. However, unlike 1967 when data was available for 'lifetime' migration only, the 1978 tabulations contain information on where people were living 10 years earlier. Figure 11.4 shows the main inter-regional migration flows over the period 1967–1978 together with the flows from each region to Dar es Salaam. Considerably more people are involved in migration than at the earlier period (Figure 11.3), and Dar es Salaam has increased its dominance as it is now the main destination for migrants from eight regions compared with three in 1967. In addition, there are very important, more localized migration 'systems' such as those in the north-east but especially around Lake Victoria and extending south into Tabora. Perhaps most interestingly of all there appears to be some indication of step-migration as evidenced by a series of 'chains', for example, Iringa – Morogoro – Dar es Salaam, Arusha – Kilimanjaro – Dar es Salaam, and Mtwara – Lindi – Dar es Salaam.

Table 11.3 Migrant population in towns, 1967 (percentage born elsewhere)

Town	No. of migrants	Percentage of urban population	Percentage born in same region
Arusha	22 963	70.0	42.2
Bukoba	5 848	70.9	68.2
Dar es Salaam	186 785	67.5	56.3*
Dodoma	17 470	73.1	52.5
Iringa	13 115	60.1	75.0
Kigoma/Ujiji	8 896	40.2	76.8
Lindi	9 285	68.2	83.8
Mbeya	8 590	68.4	64.5
Morogoro	17 426	68.0	73.3
Moshi	18 833	70.0	60.7
Mtwara/Mikindani	12 693	61.5	81.3
Musoma	11 306	72.7	67.5
Mwanza	20 913	59.2	44.0
Tabora	12 754	59.6	63.3
Tanga	39 975	64.7	71.4
Zanzibar	58 140	84.7	84.2

* Assuming that Dar es Salaam is within 'Coast' region.
If Dar es Salaam is classified as a region in itself the figure is 32.5%.

(Source: Census of Tanzania, 1967)

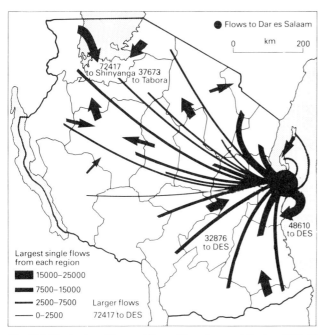

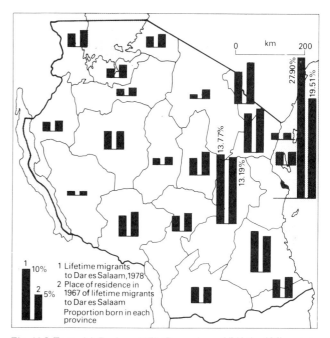

Table 11.4 Cohort survival for 16 largest towns: Age group 5–14 (1967) – 15–24 (1977).

Town	No. in 1967	No. in 1977	'Apparent' migration gain/loss*
Arusha	6 580	15 554	+8 974
Bukoba	1 519	5 804	+4 285
Dar es Salaam	49 289	171 183	+121 894
Dodoma	4 655	11 835	+7 180
Iringa	5 477	13 873	+8 396
Kigoma	4 944	9 757	+4 813
Lindi	2 594	5 967	+3 373
Mbeya	2 949	17 928	+14 979
Morogoro	5 253	14 241	+8 988
Moshi	5 344	14 115	+8 771
Mtwara	3 479	9 757	+6 278
Musoma	3 294	7 526	+4 232
Mwanza	6 674	27 055	+20 381
Tabora	4 436	14 675	+10 239
Tanga	12 965	22 327	+9 362
Zanzibar	14 727	21 140	+6 413

* Assuming no deaths

(Sources: Census of Tanzania, 1967 and 1978)

Fig. 11.4 Destination of Largest Migrant Flows from each Region, 1967–78 and Number of Migrants to Dar es Salaam from each Region, 1967–78

One set of data which is available for urban areas for both 1967 and 1978 concerns the age structure of their populations. This enables us to make some indirect observations about migration and change over the inter-censal period. In most urban areas in 1967 mature males (aged 20–49) dominated the age structure. In the four towns of Dar es Salaam, Mwanza, Mbeya and Iringa they constituted 29.3%, 27.7%, 22.2% and 21.6% respectively. Females in the same age group constituted only 20.2%, 19.4%, 19.1% and 18.0%. Comparison between 1967 and 1978 is best achieved by applying a simple cohort-survival method to the data. If there are, for example, 3000 males in Mwanza in the 0–9 age group in 1967, then ten years later – all things being equal – we would expect 3000 males in the 10–19 age group. Any surplus or deficit may be explained by either deaths or in-or-out-migration.

Even in a poor Third World country such as Tanzania the former is unlikely to be of major significance after the first five years of life (except in circumstances of major epidemics or famine), therefore taking the 5–14 age range for 1967 and comparing it with the 15–24 age range for 1978 for each urban area should enable us to make some tentative observations about migrations. Table 11.4 shows the data for the 16 largest towns. It is obvious that the death rate would pose a serious obstacle to this analysis only if, after ignoring deaths, the 'apparent' migration were negative. The very high positive figures in Table 11.4 indicate that the surplus population in this age cohort can only be due to in-migration. Whilst the movement into Dar es Salaam appears to be huge, it is again clear that provincial centres are also significant targets for migrants. What remains problematic is the extent to which they are terminal destinations or temporary ones. The migration data available for Dar es Salaam city throws a little light on this issue.

The 1978 census gives information both on the birthplace and place of residence in 1967 of all residents of Dar es Salaam. This provides tentative evidence of step-migration as it enables us to calculate the number of migrants who had been born somewhere else, were living in, say, Dodoma region in 1967, but had moved to Dar es Salaam by 1978. Figure 11.5 indicates the significance of this step-migration has occurred

when the right-hand column is greater than the left. As we would expect, step-migration is not as significant in most of the regions immediately adjacent to Dar es Salaam. It is particularly marked in those regions which possess larger regional centres such as Mwanza, Dodoma, West Lake (Bukoba), and Kilimanjaro (Moshi). It would appear, therefore, that step-migration does exist but is more marked in some regions than in others. Indeed, comparing Figures 11.3 and 11.4 it would appear from the longer distance and greater flows that direct migration into Dar es Salaam has increased. By 1978, in addition to being the major destination of flows from eight regions, Dar es Salaam is the second most important destination for a further five regions.

There is also some indirect evidence of return migration or circular migration (type E). For example, in Kilimanjaro in 1977 there were 4117 people who had been living in Dar es Salaam in 1967. Of these, 3007 had been born in Dar es Salaam, therefore some 1110 had been born elsewhere, moved to Dar es Salaam by 1967, but by 1977 were living in

Fig. 11.5 Tanzania's Regions, 1978: Comparison of 'Lifetime' Migrants to Dar es Salaam and 1967 Place of Residence of Migrants to Dar es Salaam

Kilimanjaro. Apart from Kilimanjaro the most significant regions for this type of movement were in descending order Morogoro, Tanga, Arusha, Lindi and Dodoma. However, the numerical significance of this category is limited when compared with overall flows of migrants.

Finally we may observe for Dar es Salaam that there appears to be a move towards rather more female migration. Whilst the proportion of male migrants increased by 160.5% between 1967 and 1978 that of females increased by 174.6%. For those migrating to Dar es Salaam in the 1967–1978 period there were 814 females for every 1000 males, a significant change from 1967.

Conclusion

Examination of the available data from the censuses of 1967 and 1978 enables us to reach the following conclusions:

(i)   migration has increased considerably over the period;

(ii) relatively short-range moves within rural areas (type A) are still numerically the most significant, especially for women;

(iii) direct migration to Dar es Salaam (type B) is apparent at both periods but appears to have increased by 1978;

(iv) despite the above, migration to other urban areas is also significant;

(v)   there is considerable indirect evidence that step-migration (type C) exists but its significance varies between regions;

(vi) evidence of circular migration may be found (type E) but its numerical significance appears to be limited;

(vii) women are less involved than men in longer-distance migration but their participation is increasing.

Our main concern has been to assess the relative significance of direct or step-migration from rural to urban areas. As anticipated, neither of these two forms of migration is applicable for all regions of Tanzania. Step-migration occurs where certain conditions are satisfied. Some districts are too close to Dar es Salaam for intermediate-sized urban areas to exert much attraction. In other regions the local urban attraction may be too weak and therefore direct migration to Dar es Salaam is more likely, despite the distance involved. Similarly, poor transport links within regions may deter step-migration. Non-urban attractions also influence population movement. The labour demands of cash-crop areas, the introduction of development schemes, and the policy of villagization have all induced substantial migration in Tanzania independent of the urban hierarchy. Finally, over time we may expect step-migration to decline in significance. As the relative accessibility of the large urban centre improves and as its social and cultural domination increases so it becomes 'nearer' to all parts of the country in both a time-travel and psychological sense. In such circumstances, direct migration would appear to become more likely.

ASSIGNMENTS

1. Using the data in Table 1.11, calculate the rates of growth for each urban area for 1957–67, 1967–78 and 1978–88. Comment on the spatial pattern of urban growth in Tanzania over the period 1957–88.

2. Examine Figures 11.3 and 11.4:
    (a) describe the changing patterns of migration;
    (b) attempt to account for these changes.

3. Using Figure 11.5 and the Conclusion to Chapter 11, attempt to account for the pattern of step-migration shown.

4. Using the text, tables and illustrations, attempt to find examples of the types of migration shown in Figure 11.1.

12 Tourism and the Third World

L A France and J Towner

Introduction

In recent years there has been a growing interest in the role of international tourism in Third World countries and the influence that it may have on economic development. Although in global terms the proportion of tourists travelling to Third World destinations is only about 17% of total tourism movements, this is a proportion that has doubled in the last ten years. More significantly, the impacts of tourism can have major consequences for individual Third World countries. At one time there was the assumption that international tourism would inject much-needed foreign exchange into the economies of developing countries and act as a stimulus to growth. The reality for many countries, however, has been that economic benefits have at best been marginal and may well have been outweighed by adverse social, cultural and environmental impacts.

In order to understand the complex influences that tourism can have in the Third World, a number of general models may help to clarify some of the essential relationships. The experiences of individual countries may vary from these general models but this should stimulate enquiry into why there are such differences.

The core–periphery structure of Third World tourism

The economic and political world structure is often viewed in the form of core and periphery relationships. The core countries are the economically developed First World nations of Western Europe, North America and Japan. The periphery countries

are principally those of the Third World developing countries. Relationships are dominated by the core where economic and political power is concentrated. Figure 12.1 shows a model devised by Stephen Britton which places Third World tourism firmly within this core–periphery structure. As with other forms of development, tourism in Third World economies can sustain class and regional inequalities, economic problems and social tensions. Thus, Third World tourism can be understood only within the context of the historical and political processes that underlie development in general. This analysis of Third World political and economic structures derives from 'dependency theory'. Countries in the Third World possess social and economic distortions due to their past experiences of colonial domination. The core nations imposed types of production, social organization and trading patterns on the periphery countries who had specialized commodity export enclaves created within them to serve outside interests. This dependent relationship has continued into the post-colonial era because of these long-term and deep-seated relationships.

Present-day Third World tourism operates within this dependency system. Tourists move from the core countries to the periphery and the control of, and profits from, these flows return to the core. This is because the major tourism companies (including tour operators, airlines and hotel chains) are located in the core. Here, they can promote certain forms of travel, influence tourist flows by controlling international transport and raise capital for tourism infrastructure projects. The inability of Third World countries to create the supply and quality of services required by mass tourism, whether it be in hotel construction and management or guaranteeing acceptable food supplies, merely increases their dependency on the core. As the development and ownership of tourism facilities is mainly in the hands of international companies, so most of the profits from tourism 'leak' back to the core countries.

Figure 12.1 indicates the main elements of the system, with a tourist enclave created in the Third World country. The hotels and services are foreign owned and serve foreign interests. Tourist movements to the resort enclaves and to visitor attractions are also controlled by outside concerns. Social and economic contact with residents is limited to the purchase of handicrafts and souvenirs or the use of local services such as taxis. Direct employment for the local population is restricted to low-paid seasonal labour in the resort enclaves. Thus a form of dual economy is created within the destination country.

The cycle of evolution of tourism areas

In addition to examining Third World tourism in spatial (core–periphery) terms, it is also possible to view its development and changing structure over time. Butler's cycle of evolution of tourism areas can be related to Third World destinations.

Butler's model envisages six main stages in the evolution of

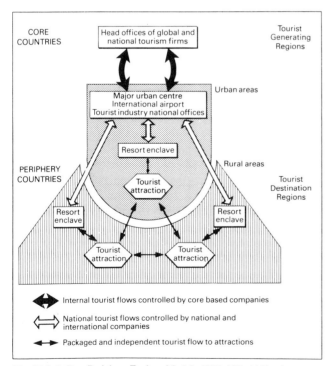

Fig. 12.1 A Core-Periphery Enclave Model of Third World Tourism

a tourism area:

1. *Exploration stage*. A small number of tourists travel independently to an area primarily interested in its natural and cultural attributes. The economic and social impact of tourism is slight.
2. *Involvement stage*. Some local residents provide facilities for visitors. Travel arrangements are organized and pressure builds up for improved infrastructure such as transport and accommodation.
3. *Development stage*. A tourist market is well-defined, partly directed by development and promotion from core countries. Local involvement in this process declines rapidly. There are parallels here with Figure 12.1. The type of tourists changes to greater numbers of packaged tourists.
4. *Consolidation stage*. The rate of increase in visitor numbers declines although the total number still increases. Tourism is a major element in the country's economy. Extensive marketing and advertising by travel companies attempt to extend the visitor season and identify new tourism markets such as self-catering or time-share developments. There may be some resentment by local people towards tourism if they do not seem to be benefiting from its presence.
5. *Stagnation stage*. Peak visitor numbers have been reached and there are growing economic, social and environmental problems. Much tourism is repeat visits rather than new visitors and 'artificial' attractions may be created to encourage new markets. The original cultural and physical environment of the area is now of little importance to most visitors.
6. *Decline stage*. The number of visitors to the area declines as competition from new destination areas grows. Property turnover is high as firms move out of tourism. Local involvement in tourism may increase as the price of facilities declines. Hotels may be converted into convalescent or retirement homes or apartments. Eventually, the area may lose its tourism function entirely.

Decline, however, is not inevitable and Butler's model contains the possibility of rejuvenation in an area where new facilities or markets are successfully developed and visitor numbers are sustained or increased. The area may focus, for instance, on specific forms of tourism such as activity-based holidays or promote new resources previously neglected.

Not all areas, of course, will follow this cycle. 'Instant resorts' can be created in new areas with a rapidly built supporting infrastructure. Heavy foreign investment is helping to create mass tourism resorts in countries such as Turkey and The Gambia and many other Third World destinations. Butler's model, however, does enable us to place these forms of development in a general evolutionary context even if the precise stages cannot always be detected. Furthermore, the model reminds us of the inevitability of *change* and the possibilities of tourism decline as well as growth. In the case of Third World countries this is especially important. As Britton's model emphasizes, these countries have little control over the nature and direction of this change and are thus particularly vulnerable to cycles of evolution, no matter what form they may take.

Case study of tourism in the Caribbean

This section will examine whether the core–periphery model of Britton and the tourism area cycle model of Butler can be seen in the development of tourism within the Caribbean.

The Caribbean is an important Third World tourist

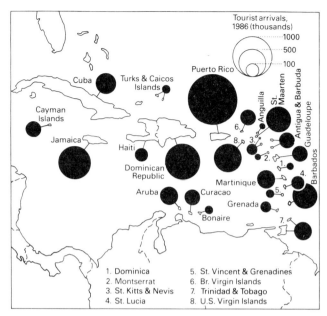

Fig. 12.2 Tourist Arrivals in Caribbean Countries, 1986

destination receiving 17.6% of all Third World tourism arrivals in 1982. Within these island states tourism is the leading industry, although its significance varies from country to country (Figure 12.2) depending upon the size of the economy, the availability of alternative natural resources and the degree of political and social stability as perceived by tour operators. Expenditure by tourists is equivalent to 80% of GNP in the Bahamas, while only accounting for 5% in such nations as Haiti and Dominica in 1986.

Britton's core–periphery model in the Caribbean

The structure of tourism in the Caribbean demonstrates elements of the core–periphery model, although there are interesting variations which show that it does not hold true in all cases.

During the early years of commercial tourism development there was little local capital available for investing in this potentially lucrative industry. Most investment in the 1960s came from overseas and a high proportion of new hotels were foreign-owned, encouraged by a wide range of government concessions. This created economic enclaves. The small amount of local involvement was usually confined to the smaller hotels and guest houses.

By 1977 almost 90% of hotels were under foreign ownership, the majority in the hands of US corporations. The implications of overseas dominance for the economies of the Caribbean island states are far-reaching, with profits accruing to the country of origin of investors rather than to the host island and its people. In a similar way the managerial posts were initially filled by expatriates, denying to local people both income and status within the tourism industry. So many of the benefits of this booming industry flowed overseas.

During the late 1970s and 1980s a considerable proportion of the hotel stock has been transferred into either government or local private sector ownership across the Caribbean, creating a situation that does not fit neatly into Britton's core–periphery model. Two factors are responsible for this trend, the most significant of which has been the low level of profitability of hotels in the region as a result of the high costs of materials, utilities and maintenance, together with the very high commissions paid to tour operators and travel agents. 'Rescue'

Table 12.1 Ownership of accommodation in Barbados, 1979 (percentage of beds owned)

Hotel (Grade)	Barbados-owned	Foreign-owned
Hotels (I)	26	74
Hotels (II)	54	46
Hotels (III)	79	21
Guest houses	100	0
All hotels	47.4	52.6
Apartment/Hotel	67	33
Apartments	65	35
TOTAL	55.8	44.2

(Source: Potter R B (1983), Tourism and development: the case of Barbados, West Indies, *Geography*, 68, 46–50)

operations involving local interests have successfully attempted to avoid the closure of many hotels and business has improved subsequently. In addition there is the desire on the part of many Caribbean nations to foster local ownership. On average, by 1986 local ownership had reached about 66%, but as Table 12.1 shows, foreign ownership remains high in the larger, up-market hotel sector on Barbados. Such a pattern seems likely to continue throughout the Caribbean, with US corporations continuing their investment strategy at the up-market end of the hotel spectrum. For example, in the Virgin Islands alone the US-owned Stouffer Hotels are renovating a hotel and plan to open another resort in 1990; Hyatt with the Ritz-Carlton Company are scheduled to open a 350-room establishment in 1991 and Marriott are investigating the possibility of another property.

There is little doubt that the selective development of specific parts of Caribbean island communities has led to the spatial concentration of tourism and its associated benefits and costs. This demonstrates the existence of geographical enclaves as suggested by the core–periphery model. Three examples serve to demonstrate this pattern.

Easy though it is to reach the Bahamas from its dominating US market by ship or by scheduled, charter or private aircraft, travel between the islands is much more difficult. So tourism is heavily focused upon Grand Bahama and New Providence with restricted movement to the outlying Family Islands, hindering the emergence here of a flourishing industry. As elsewhere, beachfront sites are favoured locations for hotel and apartment construction, with relatively little development in the interior of the islands.

Such a coastal focus is also notable in both Jamaica and Barbados. In the former, three major centres, in addition to the

capital, Kingston, together attracted 82% of all tourists in 1986. Montego Bay (39%) Ocho Rios (28%) and Negril (15%) are all situated along the north and west coasts of the island where extensive beaches, with associated facilities, are supplemented by a range of highly developed and well-advertised visitor attractions in the immediate hinterland (Figure 12.3).

Barbados has sought to develop its major tourist facilities along the sheltered Caribbean coast, attempting to preserve the more rugged Atlantic area for its scenic qualities. Part of the planning strategy here has been to segregate the different socio-economic groups of visitors into distinct areas. South-east of the capital, Bridgetown, the coast has been developed with low-priced high-density accommodation, while the St James coast to the north has been designated for the higher-priced luxury hotels. Both markets are served by a mixture of foreign and locally owned establishments. This segregation is accentuated in both temporal and structural terms as the traditional market remains strong during the more expensive winter months, and contrasts with the rapid expansion of charter flights in the summer of 1989 as more people 'trade-up' from Mediterranean destinations.

Butler's model in the Caribbean

Changes in the pattern of tourism over time (Table 12.2) have brought changes that can be related to Butler's model of the tourism area cycle of development. Demand for holidays in the Caribbean began on islands like Jamaica early in the nineteenth century. Small numbers of wealthy, often elderly tourists chose to visit this exotic, largely English-speaking area that could offer a favourable climate, particularly during the winter months. These wealthy, white visitors remained physically isolated from the local poor, black communities. This type of tourism lasted for many years in the islands of the Caribbean. It encompasses the first and second stages of Butler's model and demonstrates that these stages may last for a considerable period of time. However, after about 1960 the arrival of jet aircraft and the development of package tour operations led to a rapid growth of commercial tourism. As tourism evolved and packages became increasingly important within the travel industry, the situation changed. Middle-income tourists sought rest and relaxation, but also came to the Caribbean to imitate the lifestyle of their wealthier counterparts. Such visitors often arrived on airlines such as British Airways, and stayed in large, predominantly foreign-owned high-quality hotels.

Table 12.2 International tourist arrivals to the Caribbean (in millions)

1972	5.05
1973	5.41
1974	5.65
1975	5.48
1976	5.77
1977	6.22
1978	6.94
1979	7.20
1980	6.86
1981	6.65
1982	6.85
1983	7.17
1984	7.51
1985	7.91
1986	8.40

(Source: Caribbean Tourism Research and Development Centre 1987, Economic Intelligence Unit 1984)

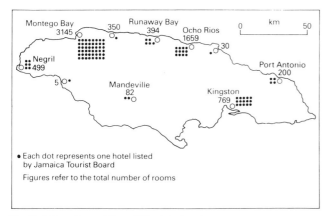

- Each dot represents one hotel listed by Jamaica Tourist Board

Figures refer to the total number of rooms

Fig. 12.3 Location and Size of Hotels in Jamaica

A number of countries, such as Barbados and Jamaica, have sought to increase the numbers of visitor arrivals in an attempt to raise income. This has led to a widening of the market through efforts to attract a new type of low-spending visitor. (Stages three and four in the Butler model.) These tourists are frequently 'trading-up' from Mediterranean destinations as a result of the strength of sterling against the American dollar, to which most Caribbean currencies are tied, and as individuals seek out new, more exotic destinations. Total income may not rise as quickly as visitor arrivals in this phase of mass tourism as a result of lower per capita expenditure, particularly on ancillary items which bring most benefits to local communities.

Two trends of the mid and late 1980s have increased some aspects of local involvement in tourism which Butler suggests occurs during the decline phase (stage six) of the cycle. The growth of low-spending summer visitors has been associated with a spread of apartment or room-only accommodation provision. This requires visitors either to purchase food locally or to eat in a range of cheaper and thus probably indigenously owned restaurants, where they mingle with the local people who benefit more directly from their tourist income.

At the other end of the scale is the development of the all-inclusive concept, as typified by the Super Club hotel chain of Jamaican origin. While this innovative form is West Indian it has led to complaints that the hotels themselves seek to isolate visitors from local people. Such conscious segregation creates physical, social and economic enclaves that are resented by local people, but which are highly successful for the promoters. Room occupancy is much higher than average as the hotels provide a standardized, 'risk-free', predictable holiday admirably suited to those Americans in particular who seek a short break where everything required is readily available and for whom the local environment is a secondary consideration. This concept has expanded across the Caribbean Basin as it has also been adopted enthusiastically by the increasingly affluent group of younger European tourists, and possibly illustrates a successful development within Butler's consolidation stage.

So in different ways West Indian ownership and some of the benefits that accrue from that ownership of tourism resources have increased across the Caribbean Basin, demonstrating that local involvement is not confined to the decline stage of tourism as the cycle of development model suggests.

Conclusion

It can be seen, therefore, that the Caribbean experience of tourism can be related to the models outlined by Britton and Butler in terms of structural organization and the general evolution of tourism. As these models attempt to simplify reality it is not surprising that interesting differences are found in the Caribbean. For example the trend towards local control of parts of the tourist industry suggests that not all Third World regions have to resign themselves to foreign dominance. Even so, it can be argued that the local population is still dependent upon the flow of tourists organized and transported by the First World.

| ASSIGNMENTS |

1. *In what ways does tourism development in the Caribbean, outlined in this chapter, match or differ from the models of: (a) Britton, (b) Butler?*

2. *Collect a range of holiday brochures to Third World countries.*
   (a) What particular images of the destination country are projected?
   (b) What forms of contact between tourists and local residents are likely for the holidays contained in the brochures?

Source Material

Barke, M. & O'Hare, G.P. (1991) *The Third World: Diversity, Change and Interdependence*, 2nd edition, Oliver & Boyd, Harlow.

Bell, M. (1986) *Contemporary Africa*, Longman, London.

Blaikie, P. & Brookfield, H.C. (1987) *Land Degradation and Society*, Methuen, London.

Britton, S.G. (1982) *The political economy of tourism in the Third World*, Annals of Tourism Research 9 (3), pp. 331–358.

Chisholm, M. (1982) *Modern World Development: A Geographical Perspective*, Hutchinson, London.

Dickenson, J.P. *et al.* (1983) *A Geography of the Third World*, Methuen, London.

Drakakis-Smith, D. (1987) *The Third World City*, Methuen, London.

Findlay, A. & A. (1987) *Population and Development in the Third World*, Methuen, London.

Kashef, I.A. (1981): The Nile – one river and nine countries, *Journal of Hydrology*, vol. 53, pp.53–71.

Lewis, L.A. & Berry, L. (1988) *African Environments and Resources*, Unwin Hyman.

Mabogunje, A.L. (1980) *The Development Process: A Spatial Perspective*, Hutchinson, London.

Mohamed, O.M.A. (1986) *Proposal for a Nile Water Treaty*, Monograph No.26, Development Studies and Resource Centre, University of Khartoum, Sudan.

Redclift, M. (1984) *Development and the Environmental Crisis*, Methuen, London.

Saha, S.K. & Barrow, C.J. (1981) *River Basin Planning: Theory and Practice*, J Wiley, Chichester.

Shahin, M. (1985) *Hydrology of the Nile Basin*, Elsevier, Amsterdam.

Timberlake, L. (1985) *Africa in Crisis*, Earthscan, London.

United Nations Childrens Fund (1989) *The State of the World's Children*, 1989, Oxford University Press, Oxford.

Walsh, R.P.D., Hulme, M. & Campbell, M.D. (1988) Recent rainfall changes and their impact on hydrology and water supply in the semi-arid zone of the Sudan, *Geographical Journal*, vol. 154, no.2, pp.181–198.

Waterbury, J. (1979) *Hydropolitics of the Nile Valley*. Syracuse, New York.

World Bank (1989) *World Development Report, 1989*, Oxford University Press, New York.